SAN DIEGO PUBLIC LIBRARY

THE SAN DIEGO PUBLIC LIBRARY · ESTABLISHED IN 1882 ·

Presented by

A grant from the
American Library Association
and
Wells Fargo Home Mortgage

APR   3 2003

Southwest
Kitchen
Garden

3 1336 06133 9389

5×|12-68/5-11
3(03-04) 8/07

Rio Nuevo Publishers
An imprint of Treasure Chest Books
P.O. Box 5250
Tucson, Arizona 85703-0250
(520) 623-9558

Text © 2002 by Kim Nelson
Illustrations © 2002 by Cynthia Miller
All Rights Reserved.

FIRST EDITION

No part of this publication may be reproduced, stored, or introduced into a
retrieval system, or likewise copied in any form without the prior written per-
mission of the publisher, excepting brief passages for review or citation.

Editor: Susan Lowell
Design: William Benoit, Simpson & Convent

Printed in Korea
10 9 8 7 6 5 4 3 2 1

Library of Congress Cataloging-in-Publication Data
Nelson, Kim, 1959-
    Southwest kitchen garden / by Kim Nelson.
        p. cm.
    Includes index.
ISBN 1-887896-41-4 (hardcover : alk. paper)
1. Vegetable gardening—Southwest, New. 2. Herb gardening—Southwest, New.
3. Kitchen gardens—Southwest, New. 4. Cookery (Vegetables)   I. Title.
SB321.5S93 N46 2002
635'.0979—dc21
                                            2002014220

To Rick, Leslie, Drew, and Lisa

with whom I share a life that offers all I need.

—K. N.

To Sheila and Rowe, hopeful gardeners.

—C. M.

Southwest Kitchen Garden

Kim Nelson

illustrated by Cynthia Miller

Rio Nuevo Publishers
Tucson, Arizona

Contents

From Inspiration to Creation: A Southwest Kitchen Garden

A kitchen garden is vegetables and fruits, herbs and flowers, paths, structures, and décor. It's the farmland of the backyard and the heart of family homes around the globe. Alternatively called a *potager,* a dooryard garden, or a vegetable bed, "kitchen garden" evokes powerful images.

What Is a Kitchen Garden?

Envision this: an Hispanic woman bends over rows of squash and chiles, planning savory *calabacitas* for dinner. A Frenchman picks baby green beans or *haricots verts*, frisée, and arugula for his cool yet spicy evening meal. Italian children collect zucchini, tomatoes, and eggplant for the piquant caponata they'll eat before tonight's pasta. In the American Southwest as elsewhere, these culturally defining images illuminate the essence of family homes. They connect a diversity of people with the common practices of working, eating, and playing together. The kitchen garden links us to our heritage, our environments, our future, and our past.

The characteristic plants of the Southwest can be grown and cooked almost anywhere, showing that in many ways the Southwest, like other regions, is a state of mind. Scent and flavor—cilantro, roasted pepper, tomatillo—may evoke a place and time and emotion as vividly in New England as in New Mexico. Historically, Southwest kitchen gardens were a main food source for native people, missionaries, pioneers, and travelers, who ate easily-stored staples and whatever they could gather or grow. Despite harsh surroundings and limited resources, these groups cultivated practices and food crops that are as beneficial today as they were in the past. For example, among Mexicans and Native Americans, young prickly pear pads have always been gathered, de-thorned, peeled, and boiled, and then eaten as a vegetable. This practice continues today.

Like our predecessors, we modern Southwesterners can develop a greater understanding of life cycles, a connection to the land, a sense of achievement, and a degree of self-reliance. Growing our own food offers opportunities available through no other activity. Gardening keeps us healthy and teaches us lessons about nature, plants, and ourselves.

Many of my childhood experiences centered on the vegetable garden and fruit trees on my grandmother's half-acre lot in Southern California. With excitement, I walked a few short blocks to Gram's house, passed through the kitchen to give and get a hug, then ran out back to see what I could pick and eat while playing. Happy memories flood back when I think of the hot summer days spent with Gram, my mom, and my sister processing plums and apricots, and making jams, jellies, and pies. In that kitchen, in that garden, seeds for my future were planted. I developed knowledge about propagation, weeding, and irrigation; and then harvesting, preservation, and storage.

As an adult I have lived and gardened in several parts of the arid West and Southwest, spending the last decade in the Sonoran Desert. Brought here by my husband's work, I've spent years experimenting and learning about the uniqueness of the desert soil, the extreme climate, and the conservative application of precious water.

The challenges are great, the lessons learned are even greater, and I still love the kitchen garden. To this day, nothing pleases me more than homemade plum jam on fresh bread, or homegrown vegetables eaten straight from the soil. In addition to skills and knowledge, the relationships nurtured while gardening and cooking are of the strongest nature. It is this legacy that I hope to perpetuate.

IN THE BEGINNING: DREAMS, LOCATION, AND DESIGN

The needs of the kitchen garden are simple: abundant sunlight, nutritious soil, and adequate water. In the Southwest the first is a given, but we must consciously manage the other two. It's best to locate your kitchen garden where it receives at least six hours of direct sun and some afternoon shade. If shade isn't immediately available, you can create it with annual vines, taller plants, or structures located west of the garden. Other factors determining location include the visual impression your garden will make, water availability, access, and convenience. If you intend to build your garden from unattractive materials, keep it out of sight, but if it is visually pleasing, as most kitchen gardens are, situate it to be viewed and enjoyed.

Wherever you establish your garden, make sure that water is accessible and the paths between kitchen and garden are convenient. Keep it as simple and pleasurable as possible. In arid regions, conserve water by selecting crops that are adapted to the region, planting them at the right time, providing some afternoon shade, and applying a thick layer of mulch. In addition to all this, water must be regularly applied, and access is important.

Once you've determined location, consider size and shape. If you've never gardened before, begin small and build success by increasing the size of your gardens as your skills and needs grow. Since novice gardeners frequently feel frustrated by tackling too much, take it slow. You may learn that, planted intensively, a surprisingly small area is all you'll ever need. For my family of five, two hundred square feet is more than enough space to grow all the fresh vegetables and herbs we want.

I currently have a circular garden, entered through an arbor and divided into quadrants by two narrow paths. Everything is accessible from those paths, and it is perfectly located just outside my kitchen. Despite this perfection, I will soon move to a home whose design and location better suit my family's changing needs. That kitchen garden, very near a nature preserve and vulnerable to wildlife, will be an outdoor room with cinderblock footers and metal posts supporting a chicken-wire roof and walls. Climbing vine crops grown on the west side will provide ample afternoon shade in the summer. In addition to these gardens, over the years I've also had four-foot by thirty-foot raised beds, traditional rows and furrows tucked into the landscape, and collections of large pots. Each technique was

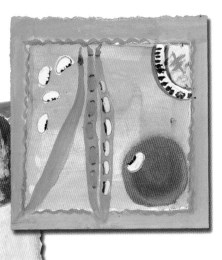

determined by location and my situation at the time. As you consider and understand your needs, let your circumstances determine your design.

Raised beds are nice for most of us, and necessary for the elderly or disabled. The elevated workspace sits at a comfortable level, and the height somewhat deters rodents from foraging through the garden. Another conven-

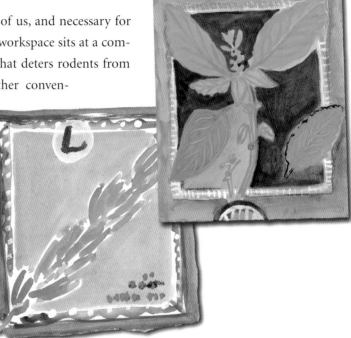

ience is the option to fill the structures with rich, friable soil rather than loosening and amending the native soil. When purchased by the truckload, this is an easy and affordable alternative. Common building materials for raised beds include concrete block, stones, brick, or heavy, untreated wood. Most of these last a lifetime, although wood naturally erodes and is affected by insects and weather. Avoid chemically treated lumber or railroad ties whose toxins leach into the soil, potentially affecting food quality and safety.

Commercial farmers still use traditional rows and troughs, but they're an inefficient use of space in the kitchen garden. If you're going to till, amend, and plant in the native ground, consider creating narrow paths that divide the space into smaller parcels that you can comfortably reach and intensively plant. This type of garden is simpler to create and easier to maintain since rainfall, water flow, and foot traffic hardly affect the layout. It's also easy and inexpensive to irrigate with soaker hoses snaked through the beds or plastic irrigation tubing and small, upright sprinklers installed around the periphery.

Although I've done it, total container gardening is only practical when no other option exists. The ground provides nutrients, insulation, and irrigation possibilities unavailable in a potted garden. But sometimes one has no choice, and a container garden is better than no garden at all. If you find yourself in this predicament, use pots with top rims no smaller than ten inches in diameter, and of equal or greater depth. Sixteen-inch or larger is even better. Closely cluster the pots so they shade one another, offering protection from intense sunlight and reducing evaporation. Choose natural terra-cotta pots that breathe and drain well to discourage root rot and fungal disease. Situate your potted garden in full morning sun with afternoon shade (the east side of a structure or large tree is ideal) and carefully plan irrigation so the soil never completely dries out.

Once you've decided on a location and design, create a sketch including not only the garden, but also the surrounding structures and landscape elements. Measure the components and use grid paper to illustrate the site to scale. When your sketch is finished, use it as a guide to mark the layout on the ground using chalk lines or stakes and string. Once marked, move through your garden space as if were already planted. If you intend to use wheelbarrows or wagons, try them now to make sure you have room to maneuver them. If you wander through the designated space and realize you'll never need that many vegetables and herbs, reduce the overall size. By moving through the true dimensions you can make design modifications before putting shovel to soil, saving time and effort. If your garden plans include an enclosed structure or raised beds, make a detailed sketch and develop a materials list to use when estimating cost and purchasing supplies. With these sketches and lists you've begun to develop another valuable tool: your garden journal.

INSPIRED WRITINGS: THE GARDEN JOURNAL

One of the first bits of advice I share with novice gardeners is to document what they want, what they need, and what they actually do in the garden. If you yearn for it, write it down. If you dream it, draw it. When you see it, copy it. Keep a record of everything you think or do regarding your garden. That record will prove invaluable as you, your knowledge, and your garden grow. I learn a tremendous amount from nature, the earth, and the garden, and my garden journal provides the medium for retaining that knowledge since I cannot always count on my memory to do it for me.

As I thumb through my soiled and water-stained garden journal, I'm struck by the changes, indeed the personal evolution, I've experienced. Thoughts fly through my head as I look at the pictures, graphs, charts, and lists accumulated over the course of many years. Trees planted long ago and shrubs first considered on a decade-old wish list have either thrived or met their demise. I've watched apple trees turn brown and die overnight, thanks to Texas root rot, and lost entire salvia beds planted in soil that didn't drain well enough when summer rains came. It's all documented in my use-worn, brown leather log. In many cases I'd forgotten details about individual plants (like the capers that couldn't tolerate the intense June sun) or garden spaces (the "monsoon garden"—a collection of Native American crops grown in rain-collecting basins) until I looked back at sketches or notes and saw the genesis of what now is. Thanks to record keeping, I know what to plant again, what to avoid, and what to recommend to a friend; and I also have proof of dreams come true. Between the sturdy covers of my notebook, pictures and words document the growth of my garden, the transformation of my desires, and the development of my needs. It is verification of where I was, and more importantly who and what I was.

My garden journal inspires me to do more, yet cautions me to do less. It guides me to learn from past experiences and to add to successes without repeating failures. It also holds hidden treasure from years gone by, like this loosely phrased recipe that I recently rediscovered, again!

A Most Wonderful Salad

Fresh Spinach	Diced Mozzarella
Diced Fresh Tomatoes	Sliced Black Olives
Sliced Grilled Red Pepper	Salt and Pepper
Olive Oil	Balsamic Vinegar

Heavenly!

Every time I reread this page, I smile at myself and try this salad again; and every time I am pleased. I've also encountered evidence of challenging times, like the page left blank except for one simple sentence: "*Help Me Before I Drown in the Sea of Domesticity*." That must have been a quite a day! I appreciate those pages and their contents. Despite its humble appearance and my careless, ragtag treatment, my garden journal is, most definitely, essential. And yours should be, too.

Choose a format that is easy to use and versatile enough to permit lists, sketches, drawings, paragraphs, and the occasional "cut and paste" project. Some gardeners like notebooks with pockets to hold inspirational articles or photographs. Others like three-ring binders for easy organization and the quick addition or removal of information. I like the permanent sequence and location endemic to fully bound blank pages that prevent me from removing valuable material at a time when I might fail to see its value. The format forces me to preserve garden and personal history.

Once you've chosen your journal, commit to using it. List or draw all the projects you hope to complete in the near future, as well as the things you yearn to do "someday." When you tackle a project, thoroughly plan it and write those plans in your journal. In addition to designs and specifications, keep potential plant lists, noting their particular needs. When you propagate or purchase plants, write their botanical names, requirements, and sources. As you plant things in pots or the ground, draw a quick sketch, labeling the plants. You'll be amazed to see how things change over the years, and pleased with the progress of your long-term garden plan.

Your garden journal should also contain specific information about everything you plant from seed. Note the planting date and weather conditions; then document the number of days to maturity and any interesting meteorological data affecting that time span. Keep track of the types and amounts of fertilizers you use as well as dates of application. Logging plant sources will help you to identify trends in plant quality and adaptability. You may learn that certain nurseries produce plant material that consistently performs better over time. Like a scientist, you will draw conclusions based on your data that ultimately save time, money, and mistakes.

Perhaps the most interesting aspect of a garden journal is the metamorphosis it verifies. Your growth and change as a gardener are reflected in the entries you add to your journal. You will see how much you've changed, how much you've learned, how much you've grown. So begin today with your current plans, and embark on a well-documented journey through time and the garden.

CREATION: SOIL PREPARATION

Now that you've refined your plan, it's time to work it. If you opted for raised beds, you've constructed and filled them with bulk planting mix, bags of potting soil, or amended native soil. If you're planting in the ground, transform that heavy, alkaline earth into fertile, friable soil. Begin by spreading an eight-inch layer of composted material over the entire planting area. Sprinkle soil sulfur over the bed. You will need two to three pounds for every hundred square feet. The bed also needs a phosphorous fertilizer (the second number on fertilizer packaging indicates phosphorous content). Bone or cottonseed meal, fish emulsion, ammonium phosphate, or balanced, all-purpose fertilizers are all good phosphorous sources. Now loosen the soil to a depth of eighteen inches with a shovel or Rototiller, or by double digging.

To double dig, visually divide your garden plot into parallel trenches. Remove the top eight to ten inches of the first trench and put it in a wheelbarrow or at the far end of the bed. Loosen the remaining soil in this trench to a depth of twelve inches. Moving to the next trench, dig out the upper eight to ten inches and throw it on top of the trench you just dug. Next, turn the lower twelve inches of the second trench. Continue in this manner until you've progressed across the entire bed, and then shovel the soil that you originally set aside into the last trench.

If you encounter caliche, hardpan, or heavy clay while preparing the soil, remove it completely. These gardening nuisances impede drainage and limit root development. In caliche-laden areas, knock drain holes through the cement-like material to allow excess water to escape. A caliche bar, sold at home improvement and hardware stores, is the most effective tool for this job.

The final preparatory task is installation of an irrigation system. I think an automatic system controlled by a timer is vital in the Southwest. A single missed irrigation during a particularly hot or dry spell wreaks havoc on small plants. In the kitchen garden I prefer one of two methods: either soaker hoses snaked atop the soil throughout the planting areas, or half-inch flexible tubing with miniature sprinkler heads on small risers around the periphery of the beds. Each sprinkler's output should overlap the next without distributing water beyond the planting area. This double coverage ensures even water application and prevents dry spots. By carefully planning and placing your irrigation system, you'll be able to walk along the garden paths even when the system is on. After the system is in place, run it a time or two to check for dry spots and puddling, and then make the necessary adjustments before planting.

Now that the soil is tilled, amendments are worked in, and the irrigation system is functioning, level the garden with a tined rake and water it thoroughly. Let it sit for a few days, and then water it again. This settles the soil, eliminates large air pockets, and encourages weeds to sprout so that you can remove them before setting out transplants and sowing seeds.

To Everything There Is a Season

The greatest difference between Southwest kitchen gardens and those in other parts of the country is the planting schedule. Because ours is a climate of extremes, we often put things in the ground at different times of year to take advantage of, or avoid, extreme temperatures. Like other regions, the Southwest is made up of several "sub-regions" that are determined by elevation and local geography. Using the following charts, identify your particular sub-region and follow the planting guidelines for the crops you want to grow. The herbs and flowers listed are those most frequently found in kitchen gardens, but the list is not all-inclusive. If a vegetable isn't listed, it doesn't do well in the Southwest; but if you're determined to try something, I encourage you to experiment. You might make some surprising discoveries! Plant things you know your family likes, and try a few new crops to expand your gardening and culinary horizons. If favorite produce items are unavailable or too costly in local retail markets, experiment with growing those, too.

PLANT NAME	10-1000 FT. ELEVATION	1000-2000 FT. ELEVATION
Basil	*Feb. 1-Mar. 15*	*Mar. 1-Apr. 1*
Bean, bush	*Feb. 1-Mar. 1 / Aug. 1-Sept. 1*	*Feb. 15-Mar. 15 / July 25-Aug. 15*
Bean, pole	*Aug. 1- Sept. 1*	*July 15-Aug. 15*
Beet	*Sept. 15-Mar. 1*	*Sept. 1-Mar. 15*
Black-eyed pea	*Feb. 1-Mar. 1 / Aug. 1-Sept. 1*	*Feb. 15-Mar. 15 / July 25-Aug. 15*
Bok choi	*Sept. 15-Dec. 15*	*Sept. 1-Jan. 1*
Broccoli	*Sept. 1-Jan. 1*	*Sept. 1-Dec. 1*
Brussels sprouts	*Sept. 1-Jan. 1*	*Sept. 1-Dec. 1*
Cabbage	*Sept. 1-Jan. 1*	*Sept. 1-Dec. 1*
Calendula	*Sept. 15-Feb. 1*	*Sept. 15-Feb. 1*
Carrot	*July 15-Aug. 15 / Sept. 1-Jan. 1*	*Sept. 1-Mar. 1*
Cauliflower	*Sept. 1-Dec. 1*	*Aug. 15-Jan. 1*
Chard	*Sept. 1-Jan. 1*	*Sept.. 1-Mar. 1*
Chive	*Sept. 15-Jan. 15*	*Sept. 1-Jan. 1*
Cilantro	*Sept. 15-Jan. 15*	*Sept. 1-Jan. 1*
Corn	*Feb. 15-Mar. 1 / July 30-Aug. 30*	*Feb. 15-Mar. 15 / July 15-Aug. 15*
Cucumber	*Dec. 1-Apr. 1*	*Mar. 1-Apr. 1 / Aug. 15-Sept. 15*
Dill	*Sept. 15-Feb. 1*	*Sept. 15-Feb. 1*
Eggplant	*Jan. 15-Apr. 1*	*Feb. 1-Apr. 1*
Garlic	*Sept. 1-Dec. 1*	*Sept. 1-Dec. 1*
Kale	*Sept. 1-Dec. 1*	*Sept. 1-Dec. 1*
Kohlrabi	*Sept. 1-Dec. 1*	*Sept. 1-Dec. 1*
Lavender	*Sept. 1-June 1*	*Sept. 1- June 1*
Leek	*Sept. 15-Dec. 15*	*Sept. 1-Jan. 1*
Marigold	*Feb. 1-Sept. 15*	*Feb. 1-Sept. 15*

2000-3000 FT. ELEVATION	3000-4000 FT. ELEVATION	4000-5000 FT. ELEVATION
Apr. 1-June 1	*Feb. 15-Mar. 30*	*May 10-May 25*
Mar. 1-Apr. 1 / July 15- Aug. 15	*Apr. 15-July 15*	*May 15-July 1*
July 15-Aug. 15	*Apr. 15-July 15*	*May 15-July 1*
Aug. 15-Apr. 1	*Mar. 1-May 1*	*May 1-July 15*
Mar. 1-Apr. 1 / July 15-Aug. 15	*Apr. 15-July 15*	*May 15-July 1*
Aug. 15- Jan. 15	*July 1-Sept. 15*	*June 1-July 15*
Aug. 15-Oct. 15	*Apr. 15-July 15*	*Apr. 1 -July 15*
Aug. 15- Oct. 15	*July 1-Aug. 1*	*June 1-July 1*
Aug. 15-Oct. 15	*Mar. 15-May 1 / July 15-Aug. 15*	*May 1-June 1*
Aug. 20-Mar. 1	*Feb. 15-Apr. 15 / July 15-Aug. 15*	*Apr. 1-May 15*
Aug. 15-Mar. 15	*July 15-Sept. 15 / Mar. 1-May 10*	*May 1-July 15*
Aug. 1-Feb. 1	*Mar. 15-May 1 / July 15-Aug. 15*	*May 1-June 1*
Aug. 15-Apr. 1	*July 15-Sept. 15 / Feb. 15-May 1*	*July 1-Aug. 1 / Mar. 1-Apr. 10*
Aug. 15-Feb. 1	*Feb. 15-May 1*	*Apr. 15-May 1*
Aug. 15-Feb. 1	*Feb. 15-May 1*	*Apr. 15-May 1*
Mar. 15-Apr. 1 / July 15-Aug. 15	*May 1-July 15*	*May 15-July 1*
Mar. 15-May 15 / Aug. 1-Sept. 1	*May 1-June 15*	*May 15-June 15*
Aug. 20-Mar. 1	*Feb. 15-Apr. 15 / July 15-Aug. 15*	*Apr. 1-May 15*
Apr. 1-May 15	*May 1-June 15*	*May 15-June 15*
Sept. 1-Jan. 1	*Feb. 15-Apr. 15*	*Apr. 1-May 1*
Aug. 15-Feb. 15	*Feb. 1-Mar. 15 / Aug. 1-Sept. 15*	*Feb. 15-Apr. 15*
Sept. 1-Feb. 1	*Feb. 15-Apr. 15*	*April-May*
Sept. 1- May 1	*Apr. 1-Nov. 1*	*May 1 -Oct. 1*
Sept. 1-Jan. 15	*Feb. 15-April 15*	*Apr. 1-May 1*
Apr. 1-Aug. 15	*May 1-July 15*	*May 15-June 1*

PLANT NAME	10-1000 FT. ELEVATION	1000-2000 FT. ELEVATION
Marjoram	*Sept. 1-June 1*	*Sept. 1-June 1*
Melon	*Feb. 1-Mar. 15*	*Feb. 1-Mar. 15*
Mint	*Feb. 1-Sept. 15*	*Feb. 1-Sept. 15*
Mexican tarragon	*Feb. 1-Sept. 15*	*Feb. 1-Sept. 15*
Nasturtium	*Mar. 1-Sept. 1*	*Mar. 15-Sept. 1*
Okra	*Mar. 1-Apr. 15*	*Mar. 1-June 1*
Onion, seeds	*Nov. 1-Dec. 15*	*Oct. 15-Jan.. 1*
Onion, sets	*Nov. 15-Jan. 15*	*Nov. 1-Jan. 1*
Oregano	*Sept. 1-June 1*	*Sept. 1-June 1*
Parsley	*Oct. 1-Jan.. 15*	*Sept. 1-Jan 1*
Pea	*Sept. 1-20 / Jan. 20-Feb. 15*	*Aug. 15-Sept. 15 / Oct. 15-Dec. 15*
Pepper, transplants	*Sept. 1-Feb. 15*	*Feb. 1-Mar. 15*
Pumpkin	*July 15-Aug. 15*	*July 1-Aug. 1*
Radish	*Sept. 1-Apr. 1*	*Sept. 1-Apr. 15*
Sage	*Feb. 1-Sept. 15*	*Feb. 1-Sept. 15*
Salad greens	*Sept. 15-Jan 1*	*Sept. 1-Mar. 1*
Spinach	*Sept. 15-Feb. 1*	*Sept. 15-Feb. 1*
Squash	*Dec. 15-Aug. 15*	*Feb. 1-July 15*
Sunflower	*Feb. 1-Sept. 15*	*Feb. 1-Sept. 15*
Thyme	*Feb. 1-Sept. 15*	*Feb. 1-Sept. 15*
Tomatillo	*Jan.-Mar.*	*Feb. 15-Apr. 1*
Tomato, transplants	*Jan. 1-Mar. 15*	*Feb. 15-Mar. 15*
Turnip	*Sept. 15-Feb. 1*	*Sept. 15-Feb. 1*
Zinnia	*Feb. 1-Sept. 15*	*Feb. 1-Sept. 15*

2000-3000 FT. ELEVATION	3000-4000 FT. ELEVATION	4000-5000 FT. ELEVATION
Sept. 1- May 1	Apr. 1-Nov. 1	May 1-Oct. 1
Feb. 15-May 1	Feb. 15-Mar. 30	May 15-June 1
Apr. 1-Sept. 1	May 15-July 1	May 15-June 1
Apr. 1-Sept. 1	May 15-July 1	May 15-June 1
Apr. 1-Sept. 1	May 1- Aug. 1	May 15-Sept. 1
Apr. 1- June 15	May 1-July 1	May 15-June 15
Oct. 15-Jan.. 1	Nov. 1-Dec. 15	Oct. 15-Jan. 1/ Feb 15-April
Nov. 1-Feb. 15	Nov. 1-Feb. 1 / April	Nov. 1-Feb. 15 / Apr. 15-June 1
Sept. 1-May 1	Apr. 1-Nov. 1	May 1-Oct. 1
Sept. 1-Jan. 15	Feb. 15-Apr. 15	Apr.1-15
Aug. 15-Sept. 15 / Feb. 15-Mar. 15	Mar. 1-May 1 / July 15-August	Feb. 15-Apr. 15
Feb. 15-May 1	Feb. 15-Mar. 30	May 15-June 1
Apr. 1-July 15	May 15-July 1	May 15-June 15
Aug. 5-May 1	Mar. 1-May 15 / July 15-Sept. 15	Apr. 1-June 15
Apr. 1-Sept. 1	May 15-July 1	May 15-June 1
Aug. 20-Apr. 1	Mar. 1-Apr. 15 / July 15-Sept. 1	Mar. 1-Apr. 15 / Aug. 1-Sept 15
Aug. 15-Mar. 1	Feb. 15-Apr. 15/ July 15-Aug. 15	Apr. 1-May 15
Mar. 15-July 15	May 15-July 15	May 1-July 1
Apr. 1-Aug. 15	May 1-July 15	May 15-July 15
Apr. 1-Sept. 1	May 15-July 1	May 15-June 1
Mar. 15-May 1	May 1-June 15	May 15-June 15
Mar. 15-May 1	May 1-June 15	May 15-June 1
Aug. 1-Mar. 1	Mar. 1-Apr. 15 / Aug. 15-Sept. 15	Apr. 1-May 15
Apr. 1-Aug. 15	May 1-July 15	May 15-July 15

The Fruit of the Garden: Crops to Consider

Actually planting your kitchen garden is a most rewarding phase of the process. In a matter of hours, bare land becomes a nursery for seeds and seedlings, full of promise for the weeks and months to come. To increase the bounty of future harvests, consider several planting methods. In my garden, I vary between broadcasting, row planting, mound planting, and transplanting.

As Ye Sow, So Shall Ye Reap: The Planting Process

Broadcasting simply means scattering the seeds across the top of prepared soil and gently raking them in to the appropriate depth, which is roughly three times the depth of the seed size. All reputable seed companies make planting depth suggestions for their seeds, so check packet backs and catalogs if you're unsure. I use this method when seeds are particularly small and in the case of greens that will be harvested early and often. If the seeds are tiny, I mix them with sand to make scattering them easier.

Rows and mounds within the confines of planting areas create the tidiest overall appearance. To plant in rows, I use a sharp stick or pencil to mark a line in the soil, and then use the same implement again to make each small planting hole. After the hole is made, I drop in the seed, gently cover it with soil, and move on to the next one. I place my rows much closer than suggested by seed companies since I don't need to leave a watering trough between them. When the entire area is planted, you should lightly moisten the soil. Use mounds in areas of the garden that offer more space to accommodate sprawling crops, such as melons, squash, and cucumbers. Plant five or six seeds in each mound.

Transplanting is instant gratification in the kitchen garden, and I always plant some seedlings. To transplant, begin with healthy plants that you've inspected for signs of vigor or disease. The root balls should be dense, with white rootlets around the bottom and sides. A root-bound plant is one that has been in the container too long, developing a root system that is tight and compacted. Avoid purchasing these plants since the top growth is often too mature for the root system, and the plants have experienced stress in their early development. If the roots look very dark or have a sour odor, they are not healthy and may transfer disease to your garden soil.

When you bring your healthy seedlings home, thoroughly soak them in water, and then plant them in holes that are the same size as the root balls. Firm the soil around the stems, making sure they are not planted deeper than they were in the original containers. An exception to this rule is tomato seedlings, from which I remove the lower branches before planting all the way up to the remaining bottom branch, allowing a stronger root system to sprout from the buried stem. Depending on the crop, I plant seedlings twelve to eighteen inches apart; less if I want them to shade one another or another crop. When they're all in the ground, I generously water the garden, and then apply a three- to four-inch layer of organic mulch, like compost or shredded bark, and water again. The mulch retains moisture and maintains soil temperatures in the root zones. It also keeps weeds from germinating, reduces rotting fruit by supporting it above the soil, and visually tidies the garden. After the seedlings have been in the ground for a few days, don't forget to feed them with a diluted fertilizer to get them off to a good start.

Basil

Ocium basilicum (Labiatae)

Native to India and tropical and subtropical Asia, basil is a bushy, aromatic annual with branched stems to two feet, and shiny, oval leaves in shades of green, purple, or red. White or pink flowers grow in whorls during summer. The ornamental foliage and flowers attract beneficial insects to the garden, repel mosquitoes and flies, and beautifully add character to kitchen and cutting gardens. Basil leaves provide a distinct flavor to Mediterranean cuisine. My idea of perfection: basil, fresh tomatoes, mozzarella cheese and a splash of balsamic vinegar.

Suggested varieties *'Dark Opal,' 'Fino Verde,' 'Genovese,' 'Green Ruffles,' Italian large leaf, 'Lemon Scented,' lettuce leaf, 'Mammoth,' 'Purple Ruffles,' 'Siam Queen,' sweet.*

Potential problems *Frost sensitive.*

Companion plants *Apricot trees, peach trees, peppers, tomatoes, and summer savory.*

Growth and harvesting tips *Space plants 12 inches apart, after threat of frost is passed. Pinch back for bushier growth. Remove flowers to increase leaf production and maintain peak flavor.*

Bean

(Fabaceae)

Fava or broad beans originated in the Mediterranean, and all others in North and South America. Beans grow in one of two ways: on small, compact bushes or on pole-climbing vines. Bush beans produce faster, and so are planted in the spring and late summer. Pole beans take longer to mature, so they are planted in summer for fall harvest. Beans are eaten raw, cooked, pickled, preserved, or dried. Fresh beans are best when picked young, before seeds show through skin. For dry beans, leave pods on the plants until they are dry and brown, then pick and shell. Beans are an excellent source of vitamins A and C, as well as calcium and iron. The plants fix nitrogen in the soil, naturally increasing fertility.

Suggested varieties
Bush beans: 'Black Valentine,' 'Greencrop,' 'Improved Blue Lake,' 'Sequoia,' and 'Slender- est.' Pole beans: Asparagus or Chinese yardlong, 'Blue Lake,' 'Kentucky Wonder,' 'Rattlesnake,' scarlet runner. For traditional Southwest dried beans, try 'Anasazi,' 'Appaloosa,' 'Bolita,' 'Hopi Red Lima,' or 'Sonoran Teparies.'

Potential problems   *Pole varieties require abundant space, and all beans stop producing if not harvested frequently. Plant resistant varieties to avoid mosaic virus, and use disease-free Western-grown seed to avoid bacterial diseases like anthracnose. Yellowing leaves indicate an iron deficiency, which is easily corrected by an application of chelated iron. Insect pests include aphids, corn earworms, spider mites, whiteflies, and Mexican bean beetles, which radishes help to repel.*

Companion plants   *Calendula, carrots, corn, cucumbers, petunias, radishes, and rosemary.*

Growth and harvesting tips   *Sow seeds two to three inches apart, then thin to six or eight inches. Plant successive crops every two weeks to prolong harvest. Keep plants from touching one another, and avoid overhead watering or touching damp leaves to inhibit the spread of disease. Pick beans when they are small for best flavor, and frequently to increase production.*

Beet

Beta vulgaris (Chenopodiaceae)

The beet is a root crop that is also grown for its tender young leaves. Although beets are traditionally deep red in color and round in shape, various golden, white, striped, and cylindrical varieties are also available. Beets grow best in cool weather, so must be sown early enough to mature before the heat of late spring and summer.

When young plants emerge, use thinned leaves, or "thinnings," in fresh green salads. As the leaves mature, pick and cook them like spinach or other greens. They are especially good sautéed in garlic and olive oil. When the roots mature, eat them fresh, boiled, roasted, steamed, or pickled. The red and golden varieties can be used as a natural dye source. Beets are not heavy feeders, so they require no additional fertilizer when planted in amended soil. Beet tops make beautiful filler in the cutting garden and flowerbeds.

Suggested varieties   *Choose early-ripening varieties including 'Bull's Blood,' 'Chiogga,' 'Early Wonder,' golden, and 'Scarlet Supreme.'*

Potential problems   *Caterpillars are fond of beet greens, so watch for them and handpick when necessary. Bacillus thuringiensis will organically eradicate a heavy infestation.*

Companion plants   *Cabbage, lettuce, and onions.*

Growth and harvesting tips   *Since the suggested varieties mature quickly, sow new seeds every two weeks to guarantee a constant supply rather than planting all at one time. The seeds can be sown closely if you intend to thin them regularly and frequently as greens, eventually allowing the root the space it needs to develop. Harvest when the roots are one to three inches in diameter. If you leave them in the ground too long, they'll taste earthy and woody.*

Black-Eyed Pea

(Fabaceae)

Actually beans rather than peas, black-eyed peas originated in North and South America and grow on sprawling, vine-like plants called half-runners that hold the pods above the foliage and require no trellising. Like other legumes, black-eyed peas fix nitrogen in the soil and are often used as a cover crop since they add nutrients, require no additional fertilization, and produce an edible crop. Economical to plant and easy to grow, they were a staple during the Depression since they provide high amounts of vitamins A and C, as well as calcium and iron. Eat the pods like snap peas when they're still small, and as the beans mature and are visible through the skin, shell them like peas and eat them fresh in salad and vegetable dishes or steamed, with butter. For dried beans, leave them on the plant until they just begin to break open, and then remove the beans to store and cook later.

Suggested varieties 'California Black Eye' is the most frequently planted variety, producing abundantly until frost. 'Banquet' is an earlier-ripening variety that matures in only 50-55 days.

Potential problems If the soil becomes too wet or cold, the plants will rot. Insect pests include Mexican bean beetles, aphids, corn earworms, spider mites, and whiteflies.

Companion plants Calendula, corn, cucumbers, and rosemary.

Growth and harvesting tips Sow seeds 12 inches apart in rows or mounds that are three feet apart. Pods reach the dried shelling stage in 90-120 days and can be eaten fresh in about 45 days.

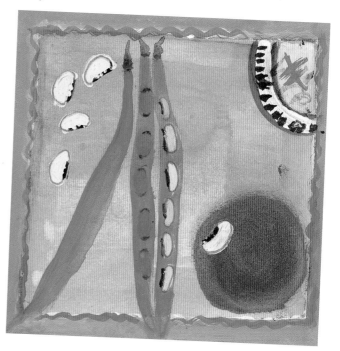

Bok Choi
(Brassicaceae)

Originating in Asia, bok choi, also spelled "bok choy" and "pac choy," is a cool-season green that grows in a head-like fashion. Probably the easiest-grown member of the Brassicas or cruciferous family, bok choi is loaded with iron and vitamins and is thought to prevent cancer. Beginning three weeks after planting, pick the tasty green and white leaves to use in fresh salads, stir-fry, or braise in butter or olive oil. The plants add attractive foliage to kitchen gardens, flower beds, and borders.

Suggested varieties　*Look in the Oriental vegetable section in seed catalogues or nursery displays for varieties that mature in 45-50 days.*

Potential problems　*Cutworms, cabbage worms, slugs, and snails all enjoy the Brassicaceae. Place collars made from cartons or disposable cups around plants to protect them from intruders, and handpick frequently.*

Companion plants　*Beets, chamomile, dill, green onions, rosemary, and sage.*

Growth and harvesting tips　*Plant seeds in very rich soil, about three inches apart, thinning to six to eight inches as the plants develop. Sow successive plantings every two weeks. Beginning in three weeks, and continuing through maturity, harvest individual leaves, which the plant will replace, or pick the entire head. Do not allow the soil to become dry, and protect bok choi from the afternoon sun in late spring, or if you sow in late summer.*

Broccoli

(Brassicaceae)

The flowering structure of broccoli, a native of the Mediterranean area, is the part we most enjoy eating, although the stems and leaves are also edible. The slightly branching plant grows to about two feet tall, producing a large central stalk and several side branches, which bear clusters of green or purple florets. As soon as they mature, eat the tight, unopened florets fresh, or steam them for a healthy dose of vitamins, minerals, roughage, and cancer-fighting properties.

Suggested varieties 'Southern Comet' or 'Superblend.'

Potential problems Nematodes are often a problem and can be kept at bay by adding organic materials, like aged manure or compost, to the soil each time you plant. Vary the location of the Brassicas in the garden each season, and plant marigolds and nasturtiums to deter the pests. Use insecticidal soap (one tablespoon Dawn dishwashing liquid to a gallon of water) to control aphids and whiteflies, and handpick cabbage loopers and other caterpillars.

Companion plants Chamomile, dill, marigold, nasturtium, petunia, rosemary, and sage will attract beneficial insects and keep pests at bay. Others include beet, carrot, onion, Brussels sprouts, and cauliflower.

Growth and harvesting tips In very rich soil that has not held other Brassicas in the previous two years, set out seedlings as soon as they are available. Keep the soil moist and heavily mulched, and fertilize every two or three weeks with a balanced fertilizer. Harvest the center florets first, when they are bright green, small, and tightly compacted, and then harvest the side florets. A heat wave will cause broccoli to bolt.

Brussels Sprout

(Brassicaceae)

A mature Brussels sprout plant has a main stalk topped with a cluster of large leaves that partially hide 50 to 100 miniature cabbage-like sprouts. Thought to be a cancer preventative, the fruit of this European native becomes more flavorful as its sugar content increases with cold weather. Eat the small sprouts steamed or roasted. I especially like them roasted with chestnuts in olive oil or butter. Delicious!

Suggested varieties
'Diablo,' 'Jade Cross Hybrid,' and 'Valiant.'

Potential problems *Use insecticidal soap to control aphids, and handpick snails, slugs, cabbage loopers, and other caterpillars.*

Companion plants
Artemesia, cauliflower, rosemary, thyme, and sage.

Growth and harvesting tips *Start from seed (125-175 days to maturity) or set out transplants (100-150 days), taking note of the long growing season these Brassicas require. Place plants 18 inches apart in highly amended soil, gently sprinkle with water, and mulch heavily. Fertilize every two or three weeks with a balanced fertilizer. Harvest the bottom sprouts first, when they are just over an inch in diameter. Yellowing large leaves offer a sign that harvest time has arrived. Remove leaves below the sprouts that remain on the plant to conserve nutrients.*

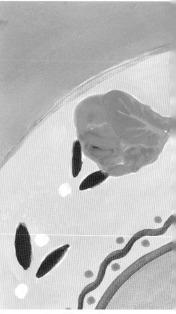

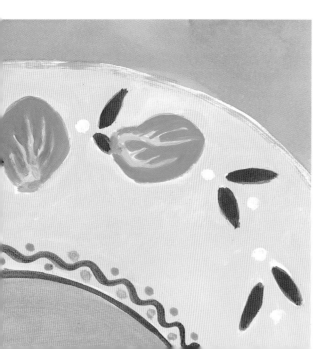

Cabbage
(Brassicaceae)

Originally from Asia and Europe, these tight-leafed green or red balls develop amidst looser, larger foliage. Colorful and shapely cabbage rows make a dramatic geometric statement when grown in sections or around edges of the garden. Eat low-calorie, cancer-fighting cabbages in salads and slaws, soups and stews, or pickled.

Suggested varieties 'Early Jersey Wakefield,' 'Red Ace,' and 'Savoy Express.'

Potential problems *Control nematode populations by adding compost to the soil when you plant and by moving the Brassicas to a different part of the garden each season. It is also helpful to plant marigolds to discourage pests. Use insecticidal soap to control aphids, and handpick cabbage loopers and other caterpillars. Prevent root maggots by ringing the base of the plant with a waxy paper collar. (I suggest Dixie cups.)*

Companion plants *Chamomile, dill, rosemary, sage, and thyme encourage the presence of beneficial insects and discourage pests. You can also interplant with beets, carrots, onions, Brussels sprouts, and cauliflower.*

Growth and harvesting tips *In very rich soil that has not recently been planted with other Brassicas, set out seedlings as soon as they are available. Keep the soil moist and heavily mulched, and fertilize every two or three weeks with a balanced fertilizer. Early varieties will be ready to pick in seven or eight weeks. To harvest, cut an inch or two above the soil level to encourage the development of small sprouting heads. Next planting, fill the space with beans, lettuce, or peas.*

Calendula

Calendula officinalis (Asteraceae)

Calendula originated in the Canary Islands, southern and central Europe, and North Africa, and it has been used for centuries to add color and flavor to rice dishes, soups, salads, and desserts, and to serve as a base for wine. The ancient Romans used the petals as a saffron substitute. In Britain, they're grown alongside and cooked together with spinach. The blossoms and greens both have numerous medicinal uses. In addition to culinary and medicinal uses, calendula blossoms and stems are highly ornamental in the garden and long lasting when cut. The flowers dry nicely and retain their brilliant color, which is also used as a fabric dye. Calendula is hardy to 25 degrees and relatively drought tolerant.

Description *Dark-centered cream, orange, and yellow flowers perch atop short, stiff branches surrounded by long, narrow, bright green leaves that are sticky and fragrant. Also called "pot marigold."*

Suggested varieties *'Kalona,' 'Orange Gem.'*

Potential problems *Very susceptible to leaf spot, stem rot, and powdery mildew, calendulas require quick-draining soil and space between plants to allow air to circulate. Avoid watering at night or getting too much moisture on the foliage. Pests include aphids, caterpillars, leaf-hoppers, and whiteflies. Handpick the caterpillars and treat the others with insecticidal soap.*

Companion plants *Beans, blue salvia, pansies, sage, salad greens, spinach, and tomatoes.*

Growth and harvesting tips *Sow seed or set out transplants in full sun or light shade. Requires little of the soil beyond good drainage. Frequently deadhead spent blossoms to increase flower production. Avoid crowding and prolonged moisture on the foliage. To dry the blooms, cut with less than an inch of stem and spread them in a single layer in a warm, dry location; or gently pull the petals from the flowers and lay them on a paper towel-lined surface. Store the dried blossoms and petals in airtight containers.*

Carrot

Daucus carota subsp. *sativus*
(Apiaceae)

Thought to originate in
Afghanistan, the carrots are
power-packed vegetables, high
in calcium, phosphorous, and
vitamin A. With bright green,
lacy foliage atop orange or
yellow edible roots, they
attract attention in the garden
and store well in the ground,
allowing you to harvest for
immediate need only. Since
carrots are biennial, leave
a few to flower and attract
beneficial insects to next
year's garden. Eat the roots
fresh, boiled, braised, roasted,
or pickled, and in stews, slaws,
or casseroles. Your imagina-
tion is the only limitation.

Suggested varieties *Unless you can
plant in pure compost, choose short or
half-long varieties, including 'Bolero,'
'Chantenay,' 'Nantes,' 'Parmex,' and
'Yellowstone.'*

Potential problems *Carrots require
light, airy soil and will not develop in
heavy, untilled ground. Using fresh
manure or too much nitrogen will
cause hairy or forked roots. Root maggots
can be a problem if the soil remains
too moist.*

Companion plants *Artemesia, chives,
leeks, lettuce, onions, parsley, radishes,
rosemary, sage, and tomatoes.*

Growth and harvesting tips *Plant in
soil that has been loosened at least eight
inches deep, amended, and allowed to
rest. Carrots need light to germinate, so
barely cover the seeds with soil. I usually
mix the tiny seeds with sand to make
sowing easier and to encourage good
drainage as the slow-to-germinate seeds
develop. Begin harvesting and enjoying
when the roots are only two inches long,
keeping at least two inches between the
plants that remain in the soil. Keep the
soil evenly moist to a foot deep.*

Cauliflower
(Brassicaceae)

From the Mediterranean, these globular, white heads grow nestled in large-leafed cups of foliage. With a vitamin and mineral content similar to other *Brassicas*, cauliflower is best eaten steamed or raw. Children enjoy dunking and eating the florets with dip.

Suggested varieties   'Early Dawn,' 'Early White Hybrid,' 'Snowball,' and 'Snow Crown.'

Potential problems   *Cabbage loopers, whose white parent butterflies you'll see hovering over the garden, chew holes through leaves and damage the edible flowers. Watch for them and handpick. Control aphids with a hard stream of water or insecticidal soap. If the soil dries, cauliflower will ripen early with immature heads. Some varieties sunburn easily if not covered with leaves or shade cloth.*

Companion plants   *Basil, borage, sage, and thyme.*

Growth and harvesting tips   *More difficult to grow than broccoli or cabbage, cauliflower requires deep, regular irrigation, a thick mulch layer, and twice-monthly fertilization. Choose varieties that develop 50-75 days from transplant. As soon as the leaves are large enough, tie them up over the head to blanch it and protect it from the sun.*

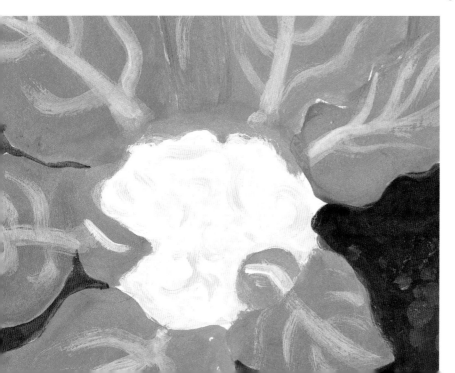

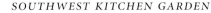

Chard

(Chenopodiaceae)

Another Mediterranean native, chard, or Swiss
chard, is literally a beet without the enlarged
root. Valued for its tasty and nutritious foliage,
this attractive, upright plant has been grown
throughout Europe for centuries. Like spinach,
chard is high in iron and other minerals. Begin
using the outer leaves when they are only a few
inches tall. Add them to tossed salads, use
them as a base for hors d'oeuvres, or stir-fry.
As the leaves get larger, cook them like greens,
saving the thicker inner core for
braising or grilling.

Suggested varieties   *For deep green and white stalks,
choose the reliable 'Fordhook Giant.' If you want variety,
or ornamental effect in the flower garden, sow the large
seeds of orange, pink, red, and yellow 'Bright Lights,' or the
deep burgundy 'Rhubarb' variety.*

Potential problems   *The only concern when growing this
low-maintenance crop is an occasional caterpillar.*

Companion plants   *Annual flowers, beets, onions, and
lavender.*

Growth and harvesting tips   *Sow seeds three inches
apart and gradually thin to12 inches apart, using the thinnings in salads and stir fries. Water regularly and deeply,
mulch around the plants to retain moisture, and apply a
nitrogen fertilizer every two or three weeks.*

Chive

Allium schoenoprasum (Liliaceae)

Originally emerging in moist pastures and along streambeds in Greece, Sweden, the Alps, and parts of northern Britain, chives develop long, hollow green leaves and flower stems from perennial bulbs that bunch and multiply in the ground. Small, purple-pink flowers form a compact globe at the top of the stem. Mainly used in cooking for a fresh, mild onion flavor, both the leaves and the blossoms are edible and are high in vitamin C. In Europe, chive tea is sprayed on berries and deciduous trees to prevent mildew and scab diseases. The flowers dry almost perfectly for use in arrangements. Bright green, sturdy foliage and attractive blossoms make chives an excellent choice for edging the garden. They attract pollinators and other beneficial insects, deter Japanese beetles, and prevent leaf spot, scab, and mildew on surrounding crops.

Suggested varieties   *Common chives, garlic chives, or Siberian chives.*

Potential problems   *None, when planted in amended garden soil and kept moist.*

Companion plants   *Annual flowers, apples, carrots, cucumbers, grapes, roses, and tomatoes. Keep away from beans and peas.*

Growth and harvesting tips   *Plant from seeds, which germinate very slowly and require darkness and consistent moisture, or plant clumps of five or six bulbs about eight inches apart. Snip the leaves any time once they've grown to four or more inches. The flowers make a mild and attractive ingredient in fresh vegetable dishes and as a garnish. Select them from different parts of the plant to maintain an attractive shape. Although chives can be frozen or dried, they are easy to maintain year-round and taste best when fresh.*

Cilantro

Coriandrum sativum (Umbelliferae)

Native to the Mediterranean region and southern Europe, cilantro has naturalized in Argentina, Canada, Mexico, Morocco, and the United States. Also called coriander, this highly aromatic herb is shiny, bright green, and upright, with lacy foliage and flat white or pink flower clusters called umbels. Many people chew or make tea from the seeds to soothe stomach upset, and cilantro's essential oil is extracted from the mature plant for use as a fragrance for perfumes and cosmetics. The minced leaves are commonly used in Asian, Indian, and Hispanic cuisines; the crushed roots impart a nutty, citrus flavor to Thai food; and the crushed seeds flavor Scandinavian pastries and most curries. In addition to being a highly usable crop, cilantro attracts droves of beneficial insects and deters rodents with its strong aroma. It is beautiful when allowed to bloom in the cutting or flower garden, filling space like fern fronds and baby's breath.

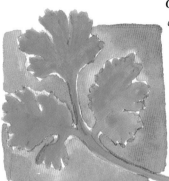

Suggested varieties *Common cilantro.*

Potential problems *Occasional caterpillars do little damage and are easily controlled.*

Companion plants *Anise, annual flowers, chervil, and dill. Keep away from fennel.*

Growth and harvesting tips *Plant seeds abundantly and begin harvesting fresh leaves when stems are four or more inches tall. Use small, outer leaves for best flavor and to encourage new growth. When the plants go to seed, allow them to self-sow, and harvest some seed for future planting and for grinding as coriander.*

Corn

(Poaceae)

Corn evolved from wild grasses in the Americas. Encased in silk and husks and covered with rows of grain, or kernels, the ears emerge from tall, sturdy stalks with long, lanceolate leaves. The size and the stature of the stalks add unbeatable visual dimension to the kitchen garden, and kids love to plant, observe, and harvest corn. Sweet corn is usually grown in home gardens, although it is fun to experiment with ornamental corn, popcorn, and miniature corn. The sugars in corn begin to convert to starch within minutes of harvesting, so no corn will ever be sweeter than homegrown. Sweet corn is delicious on the cob, freshly cut off, creamed, or frozen. Dry popcorn ears on the stalk, remove, and store in a tightly closed container. To pop, place the entire ear in a brown bag and cook on high for four to five minutes in the microwave. Ornamental corn is also dried on the stalk and harvested for decoration.

Suggested varieties 'Golden Bantam,' 'Honeycomb,' 'Kandy Korn,' 'Navajo Blue,' 'Rainbow Dry Corn,' 'Silver Princess,' and 'Strawberry Popcorn.'

Potential problems The only real threat to a corn crop is the corn earworm. To battle this pest, apply a drop or two of mineral oil inside the tip of each ear about a week after silks appear.

Companion plants Beans, broccoli, Brussels sprouts, cabbage, cucumbers, melons, nasturtiums, peas, pumpkins, squash, and sunflowers.

Growth and harvesting tips

Corn relies on the wind for even pollination and must be planted in clusters or series of rows that are three feet apart. Sow seeds a foot apart and provide abundant water. When the stalks reach 12-18 inches, fertilize with a nitrogen source; repeat when they reach 24-36 inches in height. Water deeply when tassels first form, and again when silks appear. Corn is ripe about three weeks after silks appear, if kernels squirt milky juice when pressed with a fingernail. If the liquid is watery, wait a few days and check again. Eat corn within hours of picking for best flavor.

Cucumber
(Cucurbitaceae)

Originating in Pakistan, heat-loving cucumber vines grow to 25 feet in length, and hybrid bushes develop a span of about five feet. Both have large, prickly leaves that shade the soil and developing fruits, and discourage some animal pests. Because they love the heat and require little fertilization, cucumbers produce prolifically, even if neglected. The roots produce a chemical that inhibits weed growth in the surrounding soil. Eat the fruits fresh or pickled. Blend the pulp and apply to sunburned skin to soothe the pain. Use peels to repel ants and cockroaches.

Suggested varieties *My favorite is the Armenian cucumber, although I've also had good luck with burpless hybrids, cornichons, and lemon cukes.*

Potential problems *Powdery mildew and mosaic are sometimes a problem, so look for resistant varieties and avoid excessive and late-day irrigation. Control snails and slugs by handpicking and setting beer-filled tuna cans around the plants. Interplant with radishes, spray with insecticidal soap, and handpick cucumber beetles and flea beetles.*

Companion plants *Beans, corn, lemon balm, lettuce, radishes, and sunflowers. Do not plant near sage.*

Growth and harvesting tips *Cucumbers require warm soil to germinate and warm air temperatures for pollination. Irrigate regularly to avoid bitterness, and cracking at the stem. For sweetest flavor and increased overall yield, use scissors to snip the fruits from the vine when they are young. Cukes grow fast, so check them every day.*

Dill

Anethum graveolens (Umbelliferae)

Dill naturalized in North America hundreds of years ago, but it originated in the Mediterranean and southern Russia. It is an annual herb that grows 12 to 36 inches tall and has finely-cut, ferny leaves atop stiff, hollow stems. If dill is allowed to go seed, small umbels of cream-colored flowers are followed by dark brown seeds, which scatter and reseed in moist areas. Dill is used as a condiment, a flavoring, and a pickling spice. I favor mixing it with sour cream and a touch of black pepper for a sauce to accompany salmon. It also complements apples, avocados, cheese, cream, eggs, cabbage, onions, cauliflower, parsnips, squash, salads, tomatoes, and turnips. In the garden, dill attracts pollinators and beneficial insects, and it is a favorite food for many butterflies in both the larval and adult stages. I plant dill seeds in my butterfly garden to fill voids left by deciduous plants in winter. In addition to its culinary uses, dill tea can be used as a *digestif* to soothe upset stomachs.

Suggested varieties   'Bouquet,' 'Dukat,' or Fernleaf.

Potential problems   *Like other members of the parsley family, dill will bolt during a spell of hot weather. Caterpillars often feed on the leaves and stems but usually require no control measures.*

Companion plants   *Cabbage, carrots, lettuce, and onions. Avoid planting near fennel, with which dill will cross-pollinate.*

Growth and harvesting tips   *When grown for foliage and seeds, plant dill every two weeks to extend harvest. Young leaves can be gathered any time. Let some of the plants go to seed, which can be stored for use through the warm months as well as for future planting. Dill also freezes well if left on the stem and sealed in a freezer bag.*

Eggplant

Solanum melongena (Solanaceae)

With large, lobed, green and purple leaves highlighting profuse lavender blossoms, eggplants are more beautiful than any other vegetable plant in the warm-weather garden. Growing to a height of two to three feet, these compact, sturdy plants add visual interest to the kitchen garden, flowerbeds, and potted arrangements. A main ingredient in Asian and Italian cooking, eggplants also are beautiful and delicious when sliced, towel-dried, coated with herbed olive oil, and grilled. Aside from their visually pleasing characteristics, eggplants deserve consideration because of their abundant productivity and long life cycle. If protected from frost, eggplants will survive in the garden for two years.

Suggested varieties　'Bambino,' 'Black Bell,' 'Black Beauty,' 'Black Prince,' 'Dusky,' 'Ichiban,' 'Rosa Bianca,' and 'Vittorio.'

Potential problems　Sometimes plagued by aphids, flea beetles, and whiteflies, eggplants will stop setting blossoms with a sudden increase or decrease in temperature. In midsummer, they require afternoon shade to continue production.

Companion plants　Artemesia, beans, lavender, marigold, and tansy, as well as underplantings of coriander, dill, and parsley.

Growth and harvesting tips　Set out transplants on 12-15 inch centers after last frost date, in rich, well-drained soil. Sow seeds of coriander, dill, or parsley beneath the plants to attract beneficial insects. Harvest young fruit frequently to increase production. Protect from cold temperatures to winter over.

Garlic
Allium sativum (Liliaceae)

Garlic is thought to have originated in Siberia, but it has naturalized throughout the world. Cloves grow in clusters to form the white-skinned bulbs from which flat leaves and stems emerge, grow six to 12 inches tall, and bear pale pink or white flowers. To grow garlic in your kitchen garden, separate individual cloves from a seed company or the grocery store, plant root-side down and about three inches below the soil surface, cover, and mulch. Water deeply when the top inch or two of soil is dry. Since garlic takes six to nine months to mature, plant it in an area that will be undisturbed, and harvest the heads when the leaves turn brown and die. Tie the leaves together, and hang the strand in a well-ventilated area.

Suggested varieties   *Grocery store or seed company garlic. For a milder change of pace, try the large elephant garlic.*

Potential problems   *If the soil is too wet, the bulbs will rot.*

Companion plants   *Beets, deciduous fruit trees, lettuce, perennial herbs and shrubs, roses, and tomatoes.*

Kale
(Brassicaceae)

From the Mediterranean and parts of Europe, kale is highly ornamental, with ruffle-edged blue-green leaves that often sport pink-tinged edges. The extremely hardy plants grow two feet tall and equally wide, producing abundant edible foliage. Kale is eaten fresh in green salads, braised or boiled like greens, sautéed in garlic and olive oil, or added to pasta and rice dishes. It is quite hardy and improves in flavor when exposed to frost. Attractive enough to be sold as an ornamental plant, kale is also very nutritious. It is high in potassium, calcium, and iron, and it provides large amounts of vitamins A and C, as well as fiber. This is an especially good food for anyone trying to improve his or her diet.

Suggested varieties 'Dwarf Blue,' 'Red Russian,' 'Toscano Lacinato,' and wild kale mix.

Potential problems Although sometimes bothered by aphids and caterpillars, kale is less problematic than other plants in the cabbage family.

Companion plants Cabbage, lettuce, onions, and ornamental flowers in hues of lavender and white.

Growth and harvesting tips Plant from seed or transplants, keeping bed moist, and mulch around seedlings. Begin harvesting when the leaves are three inches long, removing outer leaves first. Keep the area free of weeds to decrease the chance of pest problems.

Kohlrabi
(Brassicaceae)

A German native, kohlrabi is a curious-looking member of the cabbage family with a flattened bulbous segment topped by frilly leaves that are sturdily supported by several strong, thin roots. Colors vary by variety, from bright white and green to lovely lavenders. Kohlrabi leaves make tasty stir-fry or greens if picked when young and tender, before stringiness develops. The root, or globe, is delicious raw, boiled and mashed with potatoes, braised or roasted with root vegetables, finely chopped in stews and soups, or steamed and dressed with cheese sauce. Like all *Brassicas*, kohlrabi is thought to fight cancer, and it is high in calcium, iron, and vitamins.

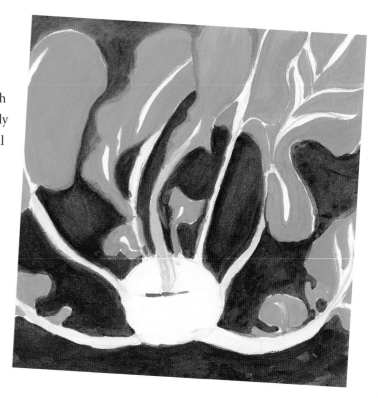

Suggested varieties   'Azure Star,' 'Kolibri,' 'Logo,' and 'White Vienna.'

Potential problems   Aphids, whiteflies, and caterpillars can infest kohlrabi, and it becomes stringy and woody if left too long in the garden.

Companion plants   Other Brassicas, *lettuce, and onions.*

Growth and harvesting tips   Sow in rich soil and harvest when small, sweet, and tender. Insecticidal soap and handpicking usually conquer pest problems.

Lavender

Lavandula spp. (Labiatae)

Originally found on Mediterranean hillsides, lavender grows in mounds of aromatic gray-green foliage topped with flower spikes in shades of deep purple, violet, lavender, and white. Individual mature plants vary in size from eight inches to four feet, depending on type and location. With its bold color and texture, lavender stands out in the perennial, herb, kitchen, or cutting garden, and it is versatile enough to use in any part of the landscape, so long as the soil drains well. It has few pest problems, demands little attention, and attracts pollinators to the garden. New plants are easily started from cuttings. Its strong scent repels insects from companion plants, and its highly fragrant blossoms and leaves make wonderful potpourri, sachets, and teas. They also are used in the kitchen to flavor vinegars, jellies, rice dishes, and salads. Lavender tea is said to calm the nerves, suppress a cough, treat headaches, and add shine when used as a final hair rinse.

Suggested varieties *'Dwarf Munstead,' French, 'Goodwin Creek,' 'Green Dentate,' Spanish, and 'Spiked.'*

Potential problems *If soil does not drain well, lavender will succumb to root rot. Often short-lived in the Southwest, the main body of the plant frequently dies in two or three years, leaving scattered, newly rooted stems.*

Companion plants *Grow lavender throughout the garden as an insect repellent, alongside eggplant and Swiss chard, and in butterfly gardens as a nectar source.*

Growth and harvesting tips *Grow in light, dry soil in full sun. Prune every spring to decrease woodiness, and harvest blossoms on their spikes before the individual flowers have opened. For maximum fragrance, harvest at midday.*

Leek

Allium porrum (Liliaceae)

Although a member of the onion family, the European leek does not form an obvious bulb, but develops a thick, tall stem topped by green leaves. With a mild, oniony flavor, leeks are delicious steamed and served alone, or with butter, cream sauce, or cheese. They are a frequent ingredient in chicken dishes, soups, and casseroles, and they make a delicious substitute in onion pie. Leeks are milder than other members of the allium family, making them a reasonable substitute for those who have digestive trouble with onions. They are virtually pest free and easy to grow.

Suggested varieties 'Albinstar,' 'Broad London,' and 'King Richard.'

Potential problems Our lack of patience! Leeks take a very long time to mature—from three to six months!

Companion plants Borage, chamomile, carrots, lettuce, onions, roses, and sorrel. Avoid planting near broccoli and fava beans.

Growth and harvesting tips Sow seeds in rich, organic soil, and water frequently, never allowing the ground to dry. They take a long time to germinate, so don't fret if everything but the leeks has sprouted. Mulch to conserve moisture, and begin harvesting when the tops reach finger height. They keep well in the garden until the heat arrives, at which time you should harvest those remaining, cut them into one-inch sections, and freeze.

Marigold

Tagetes erecta, T. tenuifolia
(Asteraceae)

Native to Central America and Mexico, the highly aromatic marigold has deep green fernlike foliage surrounding warm-colored flowers atop short, erect stems. In the garden, marigolds add vibrant yellows, oranges, and reds to the color palette while discouraging fungus and wilts, and repelling insects, including aphids, black fly, cabbage worms, nematodes, slugs, tomato hornworms, and whiteflies. In addition to their beauty and pest-deterrent properties, marigolds germinate quickly and easily, making them an excellent flower for children to propagate. They also reseed if allowed to do so, creating lovely, naturalized spots in the garden that attract butterflies and beneficial hoverflies. The petals are edible but too strong for average taste buds.

Suggested varieties 'First Lady,' 'Gem Mix,' 'Sunset Giants,' and 'Yellow Boy.'

Potential problems *Generally problem-free.*

Companion plants *Cabbages, potatoes, vinca, and warm-weather vegetables and herbs.*

Growth and harvesting tips *Plant when the soil temperature is 70 degrees or higher. Marigolds will germinate and sprout in a few days. Deadhead regularly to increase flower production, tossing the spent blossoms in the garden to reseed.*

Marjoram

Origanum majorana (Labiatae)

Native to North Africa and Southeast Asia and naturalized in the Mediterranean, marjoram is a tender perennial often grown as an annual. Oval, fuzzy green leaves on short, square stems create a dense mat that blooms with small white or pink flower spikes. Historically, marjoram has been used medicinally for indigestion, and as an antifungal and antioxidant. French, Italian, and Portuguese recipes often call for marjoram, whose flavor is reminiscent of oregano tinged with balsam. German sausage recipes also include marjoram. Unlike most herbs, dried marjoram is just as flavorful as fresh, making it an excellent choice for preservation and storage. In the garden, marjoram is an excellent filler plant for full-sun locations, and its flowers and dried sprigs are often added to floral arrangements and culinary wreaths.

Suggested varieties Italian, Sicilian, or sweet.

Potential problems These seeds are slow to germinate, so they should be started indoors. Like most of the Mediterranean natives, marjoram will rot if planted in soil that remains wet.

Companion plants Annual flowers, vegetables, and other herbs.

Growth and harvesting tips After the last frost date, set out in well-drained, full-sun location. Water deeply and infrequently and pinch plants back to encourage bushiness. After blooming, cut the entire plant to one inch above the ground.

Melon

Cucumis melo, Citrullis lanatus
(Cucurbitaceae)

Melons originated in Africa
and spread across the world,
developing into a huge number
of varieties thanks to natural
selection and careful propaga-
tion. Colorful bulbous fruits in shades of
green, orange, tan, and yellow are borne on
long trailing vines with deeply lobed fan-like
leaves that require ample garden space. Eat the
naturally sweet, high-fiber flesh alone, in fruit
salads, or with seafood, chicken, or pork; and
pickle the rinds.

Suggested varieties *When considering the
melon family, we envision cantaloupes,
honeydews, and traditional watermelons
because these easily-picked and easily-shipped
varieties make economic sense to commercial growers. However, since we can leave
them on the vine until fully ripe in our own
gardens, sweet and juicy fruits of varying
flavors and textures are available to the home gardener.*

Cantaloupes *'Ambrosia,' 'Solid Gold,' 'Sweet 'n' Early,' and
'Top Mark.'*

Watermelons *'Black Diamond,' 'Desert King,' 'Moons and
Stars,' 'Orange Sunshine,' 'Sugar Baby,' and 'Quetzali.'*

Other melons *Ananas, Canary, Charentais, Crenshaw,
Galia, 'Gold Rind' honeydew, and green flesh honeydew.*

Potential problems *Control cucumber beetles with
diatomaceous earth. Since fungus can be a problem, plant
where sunshine is abundant, and water early in the day. If
you notice mold on the leaves, immediately spray with a
food-safe fungicide or a tablespoon of baking soda dissolved
in a quart of water.*

Companion plant *Corn, lemon balm, and morning glories.*

Growth and harvesting tips *Melons require plenty of
room to sprawl in full sun. Plant six to eight seeds two
inches apart in small mounds that are about six feet apart.
Thin the seedlings to three plants per hill. Mulch heavily
beneath the vines and the developing fruits to conserve
moisture and prevent insect damage and rot.*

Mexican Tarragon
Tagetes lucida (Asteraceae)

Native to Central America and Mexico, the perennial Mexican tarragon is often grown as an annual, producing narrow, uncut leaves along unbranched stems that grow three feet tall. Mexican tarragon attracts butterflies and hoverflies and discourages pests including aphids, fungus gnats, nematodes, and whiteflies. This aggressively-growing member of the aster or marigold family adds verdant green color and interesting texture to the herb or kitchen garden and is an excellent substitute in any recipe calling for that traditional licorice flavor of French or Russian tarragon.

Suggested varieties   *Mexican tarragon or Mexican marigold.*

Potential problems   *Generally problem free.*

Companion plants   *Cabbage, potatoes, sage, salad greens, and any warm-weather vegetables or herbs.*

Growth and harvesting tips
Sow seeds or plant transplants in a sunny location after the last frost date. Water regularly to establish, less often as plants mature. Harvest leaves and stems regularly, and cut the plant back to the ground after it flowers, to encourage new growth.

Mint

Mentha spp. (Labiatae)

The mints are thought to be indigenous to Asia and Europe, with some types originating in Australia and South Africa. Demonstrating their tenacity and invasive nature, they aggressively naturalized throughout North and South America, growing in abundance wherever soil and moisture combined to encourage them. Among the most frequently utilized herbs, mints have served in temple rites and as tithes, as cleaning agents and as a symbol of hospitality, cosmetically as an astringent and breath freshener, and medicinally to cure hoarse throats, hiccups, stomach upsets, headaches, heartburn, insomnia, and muscle spasms. In the kitchen, mint adds flavor to spring lamb, fish, eggplant, white beans, lentils, cracked wheat, fruit salads and drinks, peas, jellies, sauces, candies, marinades, and the classic Kentucky bourbon mint julep. Mint is also the classic garnish for a tall, cool glass of iced tea or fresh-squeezed lemonade.

Suggested varieties *Apple mint, Bergamot mint, chocolate mint, Corsican mint, curly mint, Egyptian mint, grapefruit mint, lemon mint, lime mint, orange mint, pennyroyal, peppermint, pineapple mint, spearmint*

Potential problems *Mint is susceptible to anthracnose, rust, and verticillium wilt. To avoid these, take care to introduce only healthy specimens into your garden, and provide each plant with good air circulation. Insects that frequent the mint pots include whiteflies, spider mites, mint flea beetles, leaf miners, grasshoppers, cutworms, root weevils, and aphids. Control all of the above by regularly spraying the foliage with a strong jet of water and applying insecticidal soap in extreme cases.*

Companion plants *Annual flowers, broccoli, Brussels sprouts, cabbage, chamomile, onions, and salad greens.*

Growth and harvesting tips *Plant in the ground in bottomless pots no shallower than 12 inches, or maintain as container plants to control aggressive growth. These tender perennials prefer shady, damp areas and need frost protection. In fact, limiting their water by using drip irrigation can control their growth in the open soil. Harvest mint leaves as soon as they emerge from the soil, and shear the plant back to the soil line when it gets rangy or overgrown. Replant potted plants every other spring, adding new soil and removing dry, dead branches and roots. Invite beneficial insects into the garden by allowing mints to bloom.*

Nasturtium
Tropaeolum majus (Topaeolaceae)

Originating in various parts of South America, nasturtiums grow on trailing vines or small, bushy plants with distinct, round, vivid-green leaves. Depending on the variety, they develop fragrant and edible two- to three-inch single or double flowers that bloom in a spectrum of warm colors. These attractive plants, whose peppery-tasting leaves, stems, and flowers are high in vitamin C, produce brightly-colored flowers that add interest to fruits, salads, and vegetable dishes and look lovely in cut arrangements. The fragrant blossoms attract beneficial insects and serve as a trap crop for aphids and whiteflies when planted with other food plants. The leaves have traditionally been used for their antibiotic property.

Suggested varieties 'Alaska,' 'Fordhook,' 'Gleam,' 'Jewel,' and 'Whirlybird.'

Potential problems Aphid and whitefly infestations are common and can be controlled with insecticidal soap.

Companion plants Cucumbers, salad greens, squash, and tomatoes.

Growth and harvesting tips Plant from April through September in full sun or afternoon shade in well-drained soil.

Okra

Abelmoschus esculentus (Malvaceae)

From tropical Asia, okra pods grow on erect, bushy plants with deeply lobed, upright leaves. Essential to traditional gumbo recipes, the high-protein and high-fiber okra pod is delicious in soups, stewed with tomatoes, breaded and fried, boiled and buttered, served fresh in salads, or pickled. Use this beautiful, heat-loving, and pest-free plant to border flowerbeds and kitchen gardens. Add the dried pods to floral arrangements.

Suggested varieties *'Burgundy,' 'Clemson Spineless,' and 'Dwarf Green Longpod.'*

Potential problems *Control rare aphid infestations with a strong jet of water.*

Companion plants *Alyssum, marigolds, nasturtiums, and peppers.*

Growth and harvesting tips *Soak okra seeds overnight in water, and plant those that swell, spacing them about six inches apart. Thin the seedlings, leaving a foot between plants. Apply a balanced fertilizer when the pods set and the plants are a foot tall, and then every two weeks there-after. Begin picking when the first pods are two to three inches long, and continue to harvest every other day for nonstop production until the first frost. The plants stop producing pods if they are not removed.*

Onion

Allium cepa (Liliaceae)

Used all over the world and throughout time, the onion is a staple in most gardens. A relative of the Asian lily, the onion's shallow-rooted bulb develops beneath the soil line and is topped by upright, tubular leaves and an erect stem that bears an umbel of flowers. From ancient Egypt, where they were worshipped, to today's modern kitchen, the humble onion appears in nearly every type of savory recipe. Bake, boil, braise, and broil; puree, sauté, and steam. All this and more lies in store for the ever-popular onion. The flesh of the onion not only adds distinct flavor to meat, vegetable dishes, sauces, and casseroles, but also possesses mild antibacterial and antifungal properties. Studies have suggested that the lowly onion lowers cholesterol levels, inhibits blood clotting, and prevents infection. Additionally, onion flowers add interest to dried arrangements, and onion skins have always been utilized to impart brown, orange, red, and yellow pigments to yarn and fabric. In the garden, onions repel cabbage loopers, carrot flies and maggots, and Colorado potato beetles.

There are two types of onions: bunching onions, including green onions and scallions; and bulb types that may be red, brown, white, or yellow-skinned. In the desert Southwest, short-day, or southern, bulb types must be planted. Bulb onions are a great crop to plant since the tops can be used as a chive substitute by removing the top half when they are still small. A short time later the immature bulbs can be harvested for use as green onions or scallions, while the remainder of the crop develops into mature bulbs.

Suggested varieties Bunching onions: 'Evergreen White,' 'Fukagawa,' 'Papago,' and 'White Lisbon.' Bulb onions: Baby pearl 'Barletta,' white 'Crystal Wax,' 'Red Delicious,' and yellow 'Sweet & Early.'

Potential problems Onions inhibit the growth of legumes, so they should be planted away from beans and peas. Thrips sometimes damage onions but tend to attack already-struggling plants. To ensure healthy plants, amend the soil, and water regularly.

Companion plants Beets, cabbage, carrots, chamomile, leeks, lettuce, roses, and tomatoes.

Growth and harvesting tips Sow bunching onion seeds under a thin layer of rich garden soil. They take about three months to mature but can be used earlier. When harvesting, loosen the soil around the base of the plant and gently pull it out, roots and all. Plant bulb onions from seed in the fall, and allow them to mature in the garden for as long as eight months, harvesting at different stages along the way. To start from sets, plant the young bulblets with the root end down and the tip protruding just above the soil line. Harvest mature bulbs when the leaves begin to yellow and droop. Bend the rest of the plant and leave in the garden for a few days before carefully pulling the plants. Lay them out to dry for a few days before storing in a cool, dry place.

Oregano
Origanum vulgare (Labiatae)

Oregano grew as a native plant from the Mediterranean region of Europe to central Asia, and naturalized in the eastern United States. This low-growing, bushy perennial develops fuzzy, gray-green oval leaves on reddish, woody stems that sprawl up to 30 inches. In late summer, clusters of small pink or white tubular flowers appear. Oregano is a dominant flavor in the foods of Brazil, Colombia, Cuba, Greece, Italy, Mexico, Spain, and parts of the Middle East. It's delicious in egg dishes, with marinated and roasted vegetables, and in pasta sauces, meats, and shellfish. It combines well with garlic, parsley, thyme, and olive oil. Oregano can tolerate high heat and intense sun, making it appropriate for the most challenging garden locations.

Suggested varieties *Greek, Italian, Mexican (Lippia graveolens), Syrian, and variegated.*

Potential problems *Seeds germinate slowly, so soak them in water overnight, start them indoors, and set out when threat of frost has passed. Oregano likes well-drained soil and will rot if its roots remain wet.*

Companion plants *Annual flowers, vegetables, and other herbs.*

Growth and harvesting tips *After the last frost date, set out in a well-drained, full-sun location. Water deeply and infrequently and pinch plants back to encourage bushiness. After it blooms, cut the entire plant to the crown.*

Parsley

Petroselinum crispum (Umbelliferae)

This biennial herb from the Mediterranean and southern Europe has Kelly green stems and sharply lobed leaflets. When the weather warms, a tall stem shoots up to support flat umbels of tiny cream-colored flowers. Most commonly used as a garnish and breath-freshener, parsley has a rich and varied history. The Romans used it to cover the scent of alcohol breath and to deodorize corpses. The ancient Greeks used it in funeral ceremonies and placed it in the wreaths given to the victors in athletic events. In the Middle Ages it served medicinally for kidney and liver ailments as well as asthma, digestive disease, jaundice, and the plague. Today, many natural digestives and breath fresheners contain parsley oil. Not only does parsley soothe an upset stomach, aid digestion, and conquer bad breath, but also it's also rich in iron and vitamins A, B, and C. If allowed to go to seed in the garden, parsley flowers attract beneficial insects including hoverflies, lacewings, *Trichogramma* wasps, and others. It also repels small beetles.

Suggested varieties   Flat-leafed Italian and curly-leafed types.

Potential problems   Parsley bolts and goes to seed if temperatures suddenly jump, as they often do in the Southwest. It is susceptible to crown rot if the soil stays too moist, and it can be plagued by carrot weevils, parsley worms, and nematodes.

Companion plants   Asparagus, carrots, roses and tomatoes benefit from nearby parsley, and it is a beautiful filler plant for color beds and pots.

Growth and harvesting tips   Sow seeds or transplant for the cool season in improved garden soil that enjoys some afternoon shade. Water regularly. Begin harvesting outer leaves as soon as they are a few inches tall, cutting individual stems to the crown.

Pea

Pisum sativum (Leguminosae)

From southern Europe, these dense, compact bushes or tall, vining plants with tendrils produce pods that are edible when young and whose seeds become the crops when they mature. These longtime favorite vegetables are eaten both fresh and cooked, as pods or shelled. As members of the legume family, peas fix nitrogen in the soil, making them an excellent cover crop for plots in need of rejuvenation. They are quite nutritious and produce abundantly if watered and harvested regularly.

Suggested varieties *'Cascadia,' 'Oregon Sugar Pod,' 'Sugar Snap,' and 'Super Sugar' are tasty pod varieties that do particularly well in our arid climate. 'Dakota' or 'Wando' pods can be harvested and eaten when young or shelled when more mature.*

Potential problems *If allowed to sprawl on the soil or watered overhead, peas are susceptible to mildew, so grow them on trellises or stakes and string. They are also favorites of native birds and may require some protection.*

Companion plants *Beans, cabbage, potatoes, radishes, salad greens, tomatoes, and turnips.*

Growth and harvesting tips *Soak the seeds overnight before planting one inch deep and six inches apart in soil enriched with blood and bone meals or cottonseed meal, and rock phosphate. Mulch heavily after seedlings emerge, keeping the mulch away from the stems. Pick the pods daily when they are two or three inches long. At season's end cut the plant off at the base, leaving the roots in the soil as additional nitrogen. Each year, plant peas in a different section of the garden.*

Pepper

Capsicum annuum (Solanaceae)

From tropical America, attractive pepper plants grow from one to four feet tall, with glossy green branches and leaves that produce numerous white blossoms followed by peppers in a rainbow of colors. Hot, mild, and sweet, peppers add special character to Asian, Hungarian, Italian, Mexican, and Native American cuisines. They are delicious fresh, cooked, pickled, or dried and ground as a spice. Rich in vitamins A and C, peppers are a healthful addition to a balanced diet. Hot peppers also improve circulation.

Suggested varieties *Hot peppers: Ancho, Anaheim, 'Cascabel,' cayenne, chiltepin, habanero, jalapeño, and serrano. Mild peppers: Banana, 'Hungarian Hot Apple,' Sonora, and 'TAM' jalapeño. Sweet peppers: ' Bell Boy,' 'Big Bertha,' cherry, 'Cubanelle,' 'Gypsy,' 'New Ace Hybrid,' and pimiento.*

Potential problems *Control cutworms, flea beetles, and tomato hornworms by hand-picking or applying insecticidal soap. To continue to bloom and to avoid sunburn, sweet peppers require afternoon shade when temperatures climb above 90 degrees. Alleviate blossom end rot, a common pepper and tomato problem caused by uneven or irregular watering, by applying a thick layer of mulch.*

Companion plants *Corn, marjoram, oregano, sage, sunflowers, tarragon, and thyme.*

Growth and harvesting tips *After the last frost date, set transplants 12 inches apart in full morning sun with afternoon shade. Water regularly and harvest the fruits when ripe to encourage new blossoms. Because pepper stems are sturdier than their branches, cut rather than pull the fruit to avoid plant damage. Harvest some fruits when they are still green, and continue as they develop more color. If plants stop producing in midsummer, continue to care for them, and they will begin again when temperatures drop.*

Pumpkin

Cucurbita pepo (Cucurbitaceae)

Related to squash, gourds, and melons, pumpkins are native to South America and grow on large-leafed vines and bushes that can cover 20 to 500 square feet of garden space. Give these slow-growing fruits on rambling plants the edges of your kitchen garden, or plant them in tree wells and lawn borders where they'll take advantage of existing irrigation. In addition to their value as jack-o'-lanterns and fall décor, pumpkins are a valuable food source, high in vitamins, minerals, and fiber. Excellent in both sweet and savory recipes, including pies, cakes, breads, and soups, pumpkins are exciting and rewarding if children help in the garden.

Suggested varieties The desert is not the place to strive for the largest pumpkin of the season. Smaller varieties do better, with less surface area to transpire and burn, and lower water needs. Some of my favorites are the heirlooms 'Cinderella' and 'Rouge Vif d'Etampes'; the traditional 'Baby Bear,' 'Jack O' Lantern,' and 'Small Sugar'; and the white 'Baby Boo' and 'Lumina.'

Potential problems Birds love pumpkin seedlings and will pluck them right out of the ground. Cover them with netting until they are several inches tall if this happens in your garden. Aphids, beetles, and borers sometimes plague pumpkin plants but can be managed organically by interpolating pumpkins with flowers and herbs that attract beneficial insects. Diatomaceous earth sprinkled on and around the plant bases controls more serious infestations.

Companion plants Annual flowers, beans, corn, mint, nasturtiums, radishes, and salvias.

Growth and harvesting tips After the last frost date and successively through June, sow six pumpkin seeds per mound of rich garden soil. Fertilize every three or four weeks for thick-fleshed, large fruits. The early plantings can either be stored or used immediately. Those planted last will ripen at the end of October. Stored in a cool dry location, pumpkins with unblemished skin keep well for several months.

Radish

Raphanus sativus (Brassicaceae)

Usually red, but sometimes variegated, white, pink, or black, the radish, an eastern Mediterranean native, is the fastest growing of the root crops. The heart-shaped first leaves emerge from the ground in only a week or two, making them a rewarding crop for kids. The French eat radishes for breakfast, the Germans eat them with beer, and we consider them an ingredient for savory salads, sandwiches, and crudité platters. They look like gems on a plate when glazed in stock with a little sugar. Radishes add fiber, flavor, and color to the diet and almost instant action to the garden, making them a must in the Southwest kitchen garden.

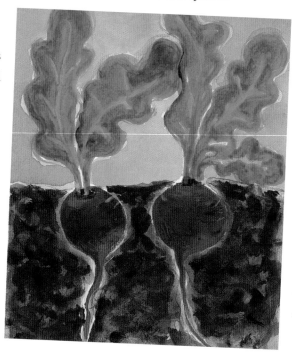

Suggested varieties 'Cherry Belle,' 'Crimson Giant,' 'Early Scarlet Globe,' 'Easter Egg II,' 'French Breakfast,' 'Misato Rose,' 'Salad Rose,' 'White Icicle.' The only variety that has not performed well in my garden is 'Black Spanish.'

Potential problems
Insects occasionally damage radish greens, but the main problem is lack of attention. If left in the garden too long, radishes get dry and pithy. If underwatered they can be hot or bitter.

Companion plants
Onions, nasturtiums, peas, salad greens, squash, and tomatoes.

Growth and harvesting tips
Sow seed in all but the coolest months, and reseed every week to 10 days for continuous harvest.

Sage

Salvia spp. *(Labiatae)*

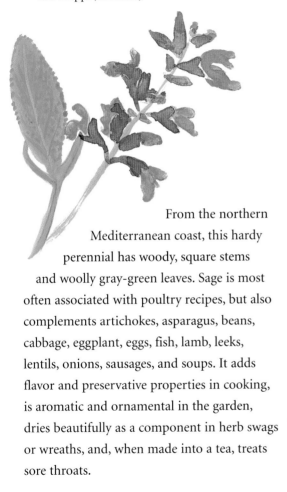

From the northern Mediterranean coast, this hardy perennial has woody, square stems and woolly gray-green leaves. Sage is most often associated with poultry recipes, but also complements artichokes, asparagus, beans, cabbage, eggplant, eggs, fish, lamb, leeks, lentils, onions, sausages, and soups. It adds flavor and preservative properties in cooking, is aromatic and ornamental in the garden, dries beautifully as a component in herb swags or wreaths, and, when made into a tea, treats sore throats.

Suggested varieties 'Aurea' Golden, 'Berggarten,' common, 'Holt's Mammoth,' purple, 'Tricolor,' variegated, and white.

Potential problems Sage is susceptible to fungal diseases if planted in poorly drained soil. Insect pests include spider mites and spittlebugs, both of which should be treated with insecticidal soap.

Companion plants Cabbage, carrots, marjoram, thyme, and tomatoes. Avoid planting sage with onions.

Growth and harvesting tips Sow seed or transplant sage in well-drained soil in direct sunlight. Water less often than most vegetables, and fertilize sparingly. To use sage, snip off individual leaves or entire branches, keeping the plant open and balanced. After it blossoms, prune sage heavily. To dry sage, remove leaves from woody branches and place on paper toweling out of direct sunlight. When thoroughly dried, store in an airtight container.

Salad Greens
Lactuca spp. *(Compositae)*

New Zealand Spinach
Tetragonia tetragonioides (Aizoaceae)

This catchall category includes a collection of leafy greens and small head lettuces from all over the world, whose colors range from white, light green, or deep green to pink, purple, and red. These tasty greens can be eaten fresh or steamed, in stir-fry, on sandwiches, or as wrappers for other vegetables or meats. Greens and lettuces are highly nutritious and low in calories, while they add water and roughage to the diet, and fresh, interesting flavors to recipes.

Suggested varieties   *Arugula, Bibb, endive, frisée, 'Indian Summer' or 'New Zealand' spinach, mesclun mixes, 'Mighty Red Oak,' radicchio, romaine, 'Salad Bowl,' and 'Sweet Red Butterhead.' Avoid those that take over 80 days to mature.*

Potential problems   *Plant mildew-resistant varieties to avoid these common diseases, use insecticidal soap on aphids, and handpick caterpillars, pill bugs, snails, and slugs.*

Companion plants   *Beets, cabbages, calendulas, carrots, cucumbers, flowering herbs, leeks, marigolds, onions, and petunias.*

Growth and harvesting tips   *Scatter the seeds in an improved bed, and cover with a quarter-inch layer of soil, since they need light to germinate. Keep the soil evenly moist to encourage germination and to avoid dry, bitter leaves as the plants mature. Begin harvesting the outer leaves when they are only three or four inches long, continuing until they begin to bolt. Entire heads or plants can also be removed by cutting at the soil line.*

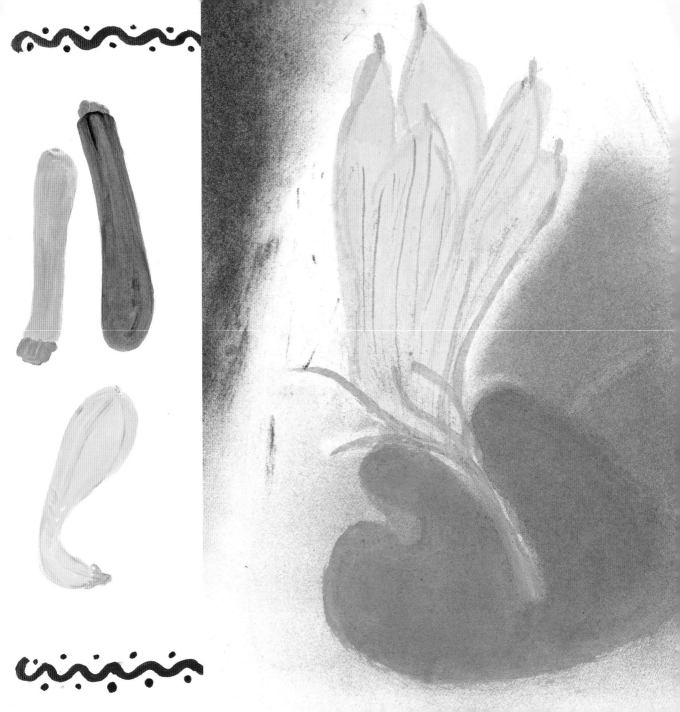

Squash

(*Cucurbitaceae*)

Squash grow on large-leafed plants or vines and vary in shape and size from small, light-colored scalloped squash to 30-pound, hard-shelled keepers. Summer squash are picked when soft-skinned and immature and are eaten or processed fresh. Winter squash are left on the vine until the skin is hard and the flesh firm. If carefully harvested and correctly stored, winter squash keep for several months. Eat fresh, steamed, baked, or pickled, and in stir-fry, salads, casseroles, soups, or stews. Prolific producers of very nutritious fruits, squash plants are among the most cost-effective crops for the home gardener. Buy and share seeds with a group to enjoy several types in a single planting.

Suggested varieties   *Summer: 'Butterstick,' 'Caserta,' crookneck, golden zucchini, pattypan, 'Sunny Delight,' and standard zucchini. Winter: Acorn, banana, buttercup, Delicata, Hubbard, 'Jarrahdale,' 'Lakota,' and spaghetti.*

Potential problems   *Thin plants to two or three per hill, or 18 inches apart in rows, and water deeply to avoid diseases. Fruit can rot if it sits on damp soil, so place a thick layer of mulch between ripening fruits and the soil.*

Companion plants   *Alyssum, beans, corn, mints, nasturtiums, radishes, and thyme.*

Growth and harvesting tips
Plant five to six seeds per hill, in hills four feet apart, or 18 inches apart in rows two feet apart. Thin to allow for good air circulation. Water deeply and regularly in the early morning, and mulch heavily. When harvesting, cut rather than pull the fruit from the vine to avoid damaging the plant.

Sunflower

Helianthus annuus (Compositae)

This hairy plant hails from Central North America through South America and grows in bush or stalk form, producing yellow, orange, or red blossoms ranging in width from an inch to over a foot. Tall sunflower varieties shade plants to their east, so I always plant them strategically in my garden. They attract pollinators, beneficial insects, and lots of birds, thus keeping the pest population on nearby crop plants to a minimum. Sunflowers attract colorful cardinals, finches, and orioles to the garden, offer shade, and produce abundant flowers for garden pleasure and cut flower arrangements. Certain varieties develop seed heads to harvest as a frugal and nutritious snack food or to store and put out as winter food for wild bird populations.

Suggested varieties 'Aztec Gold,' 'Del Sol,' 'Giant Graystripe,' 'Russian Mammoth,' 'Sunbeam,' 'Sundrops,' 'Sunspot,' 'Super Snack,' 'Tangina,' and 'Valentine.'

Potential problems *Lace bugs frequent my sunflowers every year, leaving castoff, outgrown skin and specks of fecal material on leaf undersides. As soon as I notice these clear signs, I wash the plants with insecticidal soap, repeating the process daily until the bugs are gone, since they can skeletonize the large leaves and destroy the plant.*

Companion plants *Beans, cucumbers, melons, squash, and tomatoes.*

Growth and harvesting tips *Plant seeds every two weeks as soon as the weather is frost-free. Water regularly and abundantly, and mulch heavily to conserve moisture.*

Thyme

Thymus spp. (Labiatae)

Originating on warm, dry, rocky banks of the Mediterranean region, the evergreen thyme bears small, elliptical, gray-green, green, or variegated leaves on gnarled, woody stems about a foot long. Both upright and prostrate varieties exist, with the former better suited to gardens where drainage might be an issue. Utilized for hundreds of years, thyme leaves are steeped in water to make an invigorating tea to treat digestive upsets and respiratory difficulties. It is a main flavor in Greek, Italian, and Sicilian foods, and it often spices sausages and sauces. As it blooms in the garden, thyme attracts scores of beneficial insects and pollinators. It dries and stores easily, retaining its distinct flavor for several years in a cool, dark, airtight container.

Suggested varieties   *Common, creeping, 'Golden,' 'Mother-of-Thyme,' lemon, silver, and variegated.*

Potential problems   *The two greatest challenges to growing thyme in the Southwest are good drainage and airflow. If plants are crowded in tight soil, they will fall victim to fungal diseases. The mantra for Mediterranean herbs is always the same: Well-drained soil and good air circulation.*

Companion plants   *Cabbage, eggplant, marjoram, nasturtiums, oregano, rosemary, and tomatoes.*

Growth and harvesting tips   *Plant in well-drained, frugal soil, and water infrequently. Thyme benefits from some afternoon shade during the hottest months. Harvest leaves and branches frequently to encourage bushier growth. After thyme blooms, cut it back to only a few inches, drying the cuttings on paper toweling out of direct sunlight. Then store for future use in an airtight container in a cool, dark place.*

Tomato and Tomatillo

(Solanaceae)

Originally from the Andes, tomatoes and tomatillos grow on bushy or vining plants, with deeply cut, multi-lobed foliage. A small, yellow, star-shaped flower precedes the green, red, or yellow fruit. Best eaten fresh from the garden, tomatoes are favorites in salads, sandwiches, and salsas. They are easy to preserve, but only a few Southwestern gardeners produce enough tomatoes in their gardens to do so. High in

anti-carcinogens, antioxidants, fiber, minerals, and vitamins, the low-calorie tomato is surprisingly nutritious. Hidden beneath thin papery coverings, tomatillos lend their lime-green color and distinctive flavor to sauces and salsas.

Suggested varieties   *Early-ripening and smaller-fruited tomatoes, including: 'Champion,' 'Columbia,' 'Early Girl,' 'Golden Boy,' 'Nichols Cherry,' 'Lemon Boy,' 'Red Grape,' 'Roma,' 'Sweet 100 Cherry,' and 'Yellow Pear.' Tomatillo: 'Toma Verde.'*

Potential problems   *The fruits will sunburn if subjected to direct summer sunlight in the Southwest. Afternoon shade, or a 70% shade cloth covering from June through August, is recommended. Blossom set and fruit set are often issues because the plants will not produce when nighttime temperatures drop below 55 degrees or when daytime temperatures rise above 90-100 degrees. Mulch, adequate irrigation, and shade can keep temperatures in a range enabling some plants to fruit all summer. If not, maintain them until September, trim them back by one-third, and fertilize to encourage a fall harvest. Blossom end rot is the most common disease of* Solanaceae, *caused by irregular irrigation, which affects the plant's ability to properly utilize calcium. The solution is simply regular irrigation. Handpick hornworms if they appear, and treat aphids, spider mites, and whiteflies with insecticidal soap. If an individual plant suffers from curly top virus or another sudden foliar die-back, remove that plant to prevent the spread of disease.*

Companion plants   *Asparagus, basil, corn, catmint or catnip, marigolds, nasturtiums, sage, and sunflowers.*

Growth and harvesting tips   *Tomatoes are not the ideal Southwest crop, so we must create a modified microclimate in order to reap a decent harvest. When setting out transplants, remove the bottom four to six branches and deeply bury the root ball and stem. Water regularly, and feed every two to three weeks with a balanced fertilizer or fish emulsion. If fruit is not setting, hand-pollinate by touching a cotton swab from blossom to blossom in the early morning hours. Harvest frequently to encourage increased production.*

Turnip
(Brassicaceae)

Turnips come from the Mediterranean. They are cabbage relatives and possess a similar aroma and flavor. While the turnip root, or globe, is most commonly considered the food crop, the foliage, or greens, are equally delicious and nutritious. Eat the versatile turnip raw or cooked as a vegetable in its own right, or as a potato substitute.

The foliage is a popular green, high in vitamins and minerals, and particularly tasty when cooked with bacon and onions. Turnips' cancer-fighting properties, nutritive value, high fiber content, and low calorie count make them valuable in any diet.

Suggested varieties   *Creamy yellow, 'De Milan Rouge,' flattened globe, and 'Purple White Top Globe.'*

Potential problems   *Aphids, beetles, and root maggots attack turnips and can be controlled with insecticidal soap, handpicking, and correct irrigation practices.*

Companion plants   *Beans, beets, lettuce, peas, radishes, and salad greens.*

Growth and harvesting tips   *Plant seeds one inch deep and two to three inches apart in amended garden soil. Make successive plantings every two weeks to prolong the harvest. Thin seedlings as they become crowded, using the thinnings in salads and sandwiches. Water regularly, and pick turnips before they get too large to avoid bitter, hot, or pithy flesh.*

Zinnia

(Compositae)

From North and South America, these brightly-colored, round flowers adorn stiff, vibrant green stems with evenly spaced leaves. Simply the best of the hot-weather cutting flowers in the Southwest, zinnias add color to the garden and to bouquets, and they attract beneficial insects, butterflies, and hummingbirds, as well as finches and other small birds. Long-lasting blooms adore the heat without fading in color or demeanor. With a vast array of colors and blossom shapes available, there is a zinnia for nearly every desert garden application.

Suggested varieties *'County Fair,' 'Cut and Come Again Mix,' dahlia flowered, giant flowered, 'Lilliput,' 'Oklahoma,' 'Prairie Zinnia,' 'Ruffles,' 'Starbright,' and 'Thumbelina.'*

Potential problems *Powdery mildew is a problem with overhead or overabundant watering. Carefully monitor your irrigation practices to alleviate or avoid this fungal disease.*

Companion plants *Vegetables, salvias, and other zinnias.*

Growth and harvesting tips *Sow seeds or plant seedlings when warm weather arrives to stay. Irrigate at ground level to avoid disease, and feed every three weeks with a balanced fertilizer. If blossoms become particularly small, feed again. Harvest flowers often to increase production.*

From the Garden to the Kitchen: Recipes

One of the glories of growing fresh food is preparing it in ways that are both delicious and nutritious. I love to cook as much as I love to garden, and I feel as though I'm giving a gift to family and friends every time I serve something I've grown and prepared. During my years as a gardener I've collected, experimented with, and adapted hundreds of recipes. With great pleasure I offer you here a handful of our favorite garden delights.

Anna's Ice Cream Coleslaw

Never possessing a driver's license, my mother-in-law used whatever she happened to have in her kitchen to create unique and delicious recipes. This, along with her understanding of the elements of good food, and her famous sweet tooth, led her to pair rich, creamy ingredients and intensely flavored, crisp vegetables. One result: Our favorite coleslaw recipe—the perfect accompaniment to chicken or ribs.

Serves 8

1 head cabbage

4 peeled carrots

1 cup vanilla ice cream

1/4 teaspoon salt

1/4 cup milk

· *Cut the cabbage into quarters and remove the core and damaged outer leaves. Using a large, sharp knife, finely shred the cabbage and place it in a large bowl. Grate the carrots into the bowl with the cabbage.*

· *Measure the ice cream into a small bowl, add the salt and milk, and then stir with a fork until smooth. Pour the mixture over the vegetables and mix well. Refrigerate until ready to serve.*

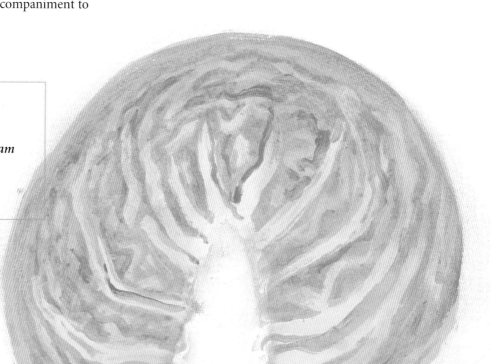

Auntie Vi's Zucchini Bread

Our Aunt Viola was a woman before her time. As a girl in the 1930s, she left the Midwest to pursue a new life in California, worked in an airplane plant during the war, married and raised two sons, and developed a reputation as an excellent cook. This better-than-any-other sweet bread is proof.

Makes 2 loaves

2/3 cup melted butter

3 large eggs

2 cups sugar

2 cups grated or finely chopped zucchini

2 cups flour

1/4 teaspoon baking powder

1/2 teaspoon baking soda

1 Tablespoon ground cinnamon

1 pinch salt

2 teaspoons vanilla

1 cup chopped pecans or walnuts (optional)

- *Preheat the oven to 350º.*

- *In a large mixing bowl, beat the eggs until fluffy, and then add the sugar and the cooled, melted butter. Mix well, and then stir in the grated zucchini.*

- *Sift the flour, baking powder, baking soda, cinnamon, and salt directly into the mixing bowl. Mix well. Stir in the vanilla and nuts.*

- *Pour the batter into 2 greased medium loaf pans and bake in the center of a 350° oven for 1 hour, or until a toothpick inserted into the center of a loaf comes out clean.*

- *Cool in pans for 10 minutes. Then remove from the pans and cool completely on wire racks before slicing.*

- *Delicious plain, or filled with cream cheese and served as finger sandwiches.*

Balsamic Roasted Root Vegetables

I first made this dish one November when we hosted a harvest party for about fifty people. I needed an easy-to-prepare, simple-to-serve seasonal dish to accompany ham. This got raves, and I've shared it with lots of friends since.

Serves 12

4 sweet potatoes, peeled and cut into 2-inch cubes

4 Yukon Gold potatoes, washed and cut into 2-inch cubes

4 red potatoes, washed and cut into 2-inch cubes

8 beets, washed and trimmed

8 small turnips, washed and trimmed

1/4 cup olive oil

1/4 cup balsamic vinegar

2 Tablespoons melted butter

1 teaspoon kosher salt

Freshly-ground black pepper

- *Preheat the oven to 400º.*

- *In a large bowl, mix the sweet potatoes, other potatoes, beets, and turnips with the olive oil, vinegar, melted butter, salt, and a small amount of pepper.*

- *Arrange the mixture in a single layer on a baking sheet sprayed with non-stick cooking spray.*

- *Bake for about 40 minutes, or until the vegetables are tender and golden brown.*

Calabacitas

Since summer squash grow so prolifically, a gardening cook can never have too many recipes for them. This one is perfect for our weekly family volleyball meets, when we potluck, play in the pool, and enjoy the benefits of Southwest living in the summer.

Serves 6

1 Tablespoon olive oil

1 yellow onion, chopped

6-8 zucchini or other summer squash cut into 1-inch pieces

2 tomatoes, peeled and chopped

2 cloves garlic, minced

1/4 cup chicken stock or water

2 'Anaheim' or 'Big Jim' chiles, finely chopped

1 cup fresh or frozen corn kernels (optional)

Salt and pepper to taste

2 cups grated cheddar cheese

› *Heat the oil in a heavy skillet, and add onions, squash, tomatoes, and garlic. Sauté for 5 minutes. Add water, reduce heat to low, cover, and cook for 15 minutes.*

› *Add chopped chiles and corn (if desired). Cook until corn is done (about 5 minutes). Season with salt and pepper. Remove to serving dish and sprinkle with grated cheese.*

Caponata

Eggplant, peppers, onions, celery, and tomatoes never tasted so good. This combination makes a wonderful antipasto or main dish when accompanied by freshly baked bread and a glass of good wine.

Serves 12

1/2 cup olive oil

2-3 small eggplants cut into 1-inch cubes

2 cloves of garlic, peeled and minced

2 large white or yellow onions, chopped

1 green bell pepper, stemmed, seeded, and chopped

1 red bell pepper, stemmed, seeded, and chopped

6 ripe tomatoes, peeled and chopped

1/3 cup balsamic or red wine vinegar

2 tablespoons brown sugar

1/2 cup chopped green olives

1/2 cup chopped basil leaves

Kosher salt

Freshly ground black pepper

› *In a heavy pan, heat 1/4 cup olive oil. Add the eggplant cubes and sauté, stirring constantly until they are golden brown. Remove to a large glass bowl.*

› *To the pan, add the remaining 1/4 cup olive oil, minced garlic, chopped onions, and chopped peppers. Cook until softened, but avoid browning. Add tomatoes and simmer for 10 minutes over low heat.*

› *Add vinegar and sugar, cook for 2-3 minutes, and then return the eggplant to the mixture. Add olives and simmer for 15 minutes. Stir in basil and add salt and pepper to taste.*

› *Serve hot or cold with sliced Italian bread and hard salami.*

Charlie's Peppers

Charlie is a giant of a man with an even bigger heart. We count on him to spice up our lives, and this recipe does just that. He likes his peppers on grilled sausage sandwiches, and I like mine with pasta … but we both like them an awful lot!

Serves 12

4 Tablespoons olive oil

6 large red, orange, or yellow bell peppers with ribs, seeds, and stems removed, cut into 1-inch strips

2 green bell peppers with ribs, seeds, and stems removed, cut into 1-inch strips

1 large white or yellow onion, cut into eighths, with pieces separated

1 hot pepper, such as 'Anaheim,' or jalapeño, seeded and minced

Salt and pepper to taste

› Heat the olive oil in a large, heavy pan. Add the pepper strips and sauté slowly, stirring often, for 15 minutes.

› Add the onion pieces and the minced hot pepper. Cook and stir about 15-20 minutes longer, until the mixture is soft, with just a few brown edges. Remove from the fire and sprinkle with salt and freshly ground pepper to taste.

› Serve as an antipasto with goat cheese and sourdough toast, atop grilled sausage sandwiches, or with pasta.

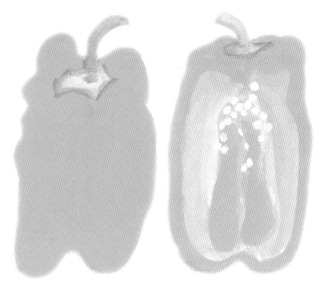

Citus Salsa

I developed this recipe for a citrus class I taught and have enjoyed it with grilled fish ever since. It's a great topper for fish tacos, too.

Makes 2 cups

> 1 orange, peeled, sectioned, and diced
>
> 1 pink grapefruit, peeled, sectioned, and diced
>
> 6 green onions, finely chopped
>
> 10 cherry tomatoes, quartered, or 2 tomatoes, diced
>
> Zest of 1 lime, finely chopped
>
> 1 Tablespoon lime juice
>
> 1 Tablespoon olive oil
>
> 2 jalapeños, stemmed, seeded, and finely minced
>
> 1/3 cup chopped cilantro
>
> 1/4 teaspoon salt

› *Combine in a glass bowl. Chill.*

› *Serve with grilled chicken, lemon grilled swordfish, or chips. Best when eaten the day it's made.*

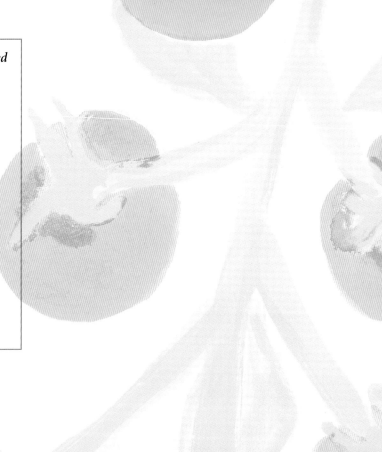

Confetti Salad

*M*y neighbor, Patti, taught me how to make this vinaigrette-sweetened mélange of radishes, carrots, cauliflower, broccoli, onions, and anything else that's ripe in the garden.

Serves 12

2 cups fresh or frozen peas

6 to 8 green onions, chopped

8 to 10 radishes, diced finely

4 celery stalks, diced finely

4 carrots, shredded or diced

1 cup chopped cauliflower

1 cup chopped broccoli

1/2 cup canola oil

1 cup white sugar

2/3 cup rice vinegar

2 teaspoons kosher salt

1/2 teaspoon ground black pepper

· *Combine the vegetables in a large bowl and set aside.*

· *In a glass measuring cup or jar, combine the canola oil, sugar, rice vinegar, salt, and pepper Mix well, then pour over the vegetables and marinate overnight.*

· *Serve cold.*

Cucumber Dip

*T*hroughout my childhood, New Year's Eve meant staying up late, visiting with my Uncle Pat, and dipping Fritos and potato chips in this, my mom's traditional dip.

Makes about 3 cups

1 large cucumber, peeled, seeded, and finely diced

2 cups sour cream

1/2 teaspoon salt

1/4 teaspoon black pepper

· *Stir the diced cucumber into the sour cream. Add salt and pepper, adjusting to taste. Refrigerate for several hours to allow flavors to meld.*

· *Serve with fresh vegetable crudités, potato chips, or French fries.*

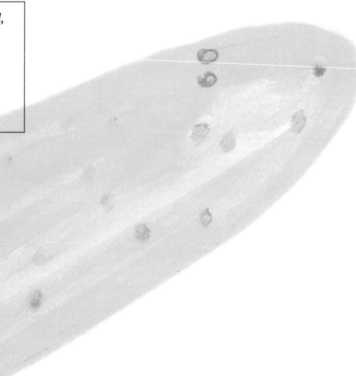

Dill and Rosemary Salmon

Served with savory stuffing, this dish graces our Christmas Eve table every year. It is exquisitely simple, and simply delicious.

Serves 4-8

1-2-pound fresh salmon fillet

1/2 teaspoon kosher salt

Freshly ground black pepper

Freshly cut sprigs or branch of rosemary

2 fresh lemons, thinly sliced

Juice of one lemon

1 cup sour cream

3 Tablespoons finely chopped dill leaves

Additional rosemary sprigs and lemon slices

› *Preheat the grill.*

› *Tear off a 3-foot section of heavy-duty aluminum foil. Fold the foil in half, and then fold up an inch or two on each side, overlapping the corners to create a homemade baking pan.*

› *Place the salmon fillet, skin side down, on the ungreased foil. Measure the thickest part of the fish to determine cooking time at 10 minutes per inch of thickness. Sprinkle the top with the salt and pepper. Lay the rosemary across the fillet, top with the lemon slices, and then sprinkle the juice over all.*

› *Place on the preheated medium-high grill for 10 minutes per inch of fillet thickness.*

› *Remove the foil to a large cookie sheet, discard the rosemary and lemon slices, and then slide a long metal spatula between the skin (which is now stuck to the foil) and the fillet. Lift the fillet to a serving platter and garnish with fresh rosemary sprigs and lemon slices.*

› *Stir the chopped dill into the sour cream to accompany the fish.*

Fresh Spinach Dip

Lots of spinach dip recipes float around out there, but they generally miss the mark by calling for frozen or canned spinach. Try this fresh recipe, and you'll never go back to the others.

Makes about 3 cups

Two large bunches fresh spinach, kale, or Swiss chard leaves

1/2 cup finely chopped green onions or shallots

1/2 cup finely chopped fresh parsley

1 Tablespoon chopped dill leaves

Juice of 1/2 lemon

1 teaspoon salt, or to taste

1 cup mayonnaise

1 cup sour cream

› Rinse the greens and remove cores, damaged leaves, and any tough ribs, then chop and place them in a large pot containing 3 inches of boiling water. Cover and steam for 3 minutes

› Stir the greens, then cover and steam for another 3-5 minutes, or until soft. Drain well, and then lay on paper toweling to cool and remove excess moisture.

› Transfer the cooled greens to a large bowl, and stir in the onions, parsley, and dill. Add lemon juice and salt. Blend in the mayonnaise and sour cream, then refrigerate overnight.

› Serve as an appetizer with crackers or chunks of sheepherder's bread.

Green Chile Chicken

Use spicy peppers, tomatoes, cilantro, and tomatillos, straight from the garden or preserved in the freezer, to turn ordinary chicken breast into an extraordinary Southwestern delight. Perfect served with warm tortillas (you can make your own!) and rice.

Serves 6

6 half chicken breasts, with skin and bones intact

1 large onion, peeled and quartered

2 celery ribs, cut into 3-inch pieces

2 carrots, cut into 2-inch pieces

2 green bell peppers, stemmed and seeded and cut into quarters

4 small, mild chile peppers, such as 'Big Jim' or 'New Mexico #6,' stems and seeds removed

6 to 8 sprigs of cilantro

Several garlic cloves, peeled

2 teaspoons salt

2 ears fresh corn

6 to 8 tomatillos, papery skins removed

6 to 8 green onions

· *Place the chicken breasts in a large stockpot or saucepan. Add the onion, celery, carrots, bell peppers, chile peppers, cilantro, garlic, and salt. Cover with water and simmer over medium heat for 20-30 minutes, or until the chicken is just tender.*

· *Remove the chicken from the pot and continue to simmer the broth. When the chicken has cooled, remove and discard the skin and bones. Cube and refrigerate the meat.*

· *Using a slotted spoon, remove the vegetables from the pot, and place them in a blender or food processor. Purée with a small amount of the liquid. Return the vegetable purée to the pot, and simmer until reduced and slightly thickened, about 20 minutes.*

· *Cut the kernels from the corn, and chop the tomatillos and green onions. Add the fresh vegetables and the chicken to the pot, and bring the mixture to a boil. Reduce to a simmer and cook, uncovered, for 30 minutes.*

· *Use as burro filling or serve with tortillas, rice, and beans.*

Grilled Summer Squash

*T*his utterly simple recipe combines the flavors of the freshest squash with the best olive oil and reminds us how perfect each one really is.

Serving size: 2 squash per person

Freshly-picked, young zucchini or yellow summer squash

Extra-virgin olive oil

Kosher salt

Freshly-ground pepper

› *Preheat the grill.*

› *Trim the ends and remove any blemishes from the squash. Slice in half lengthwise and lay on a tray, cut side up.*

› *Generously drizzle with olive oil, and then sprinkle with salt and pepper.*

› *Use tongs to place the squash on a grill over medium heat, skin side down. Cook for 4-6 minutes or until the skin has medium-dark grill marks and the flesh begins to soften. Turn the squash and cook 4-6 minutes until tender-crisp.*

Insalata Caprese

A favorite summertime snack of my son's, this southern Italian salad is absolutely the best use of sun-warm tomatoes and fresh basil.

Serves 6

Juice of one lemon

3 Tablespoons chopped basil leaves

1 clove garlic, peeled and minced

3 Tablespoons balsamic vinegar

6 Tablespoons extra-virgin olive oil

1/4 teaspoon kosher salt

1/4 teaspoon freshly ground black pepper

6 ripe tomatoes, sliced 1/2-inch thick

Whole basil leaves

8 ounces fresh mozzarella cheese, rinsed and sliced 1/2-inch thick

1 Tablespoon capers (optional)

Extra basil sprigs

· *In a blender jar, make vinaigrette by combining lemon juice, chopped basil, minced garlic, vinegar, olive oil, salt, and pepper. Blend until smooth.*

· *Alternate overlapping tomato slices, whole basil leaves, and mozzarella slices on a serving platter. Drizzle with the vinaigrette, sprinkle with capers, and garnish with sprigs of basil.*

· *Serve with warm bread and additional olive oil for dipping.*

Mom's Plum Jam (or the Next Best Thing)

*E*ach year I ask my mom for the same birthday gift … homemade plum jam. I've included a recipe here for a simple, and perhaps silly, reason: It is my very favorite jam. Mine's not as good as hers, but it'll do when the best runs out!

Makes about 4 cups per batch

4-5 pounds of fresh plums (I prefer Santa Rosa)
1 cup sugar for each cup of fruit pulp

First prepare the jars:

1. Jars must be free of chips or cracks.

2. Wash them in soapy water and rinse well.

3. Put a folded dish towel in the bottom of a large pot to prevent breakage, and then set the clean jars in the pot and cover them with hot water. Bring to a boil.

4. Boil for 15 minutes, reduce the fire to low, and let the jars stand in the pan.

5. A few minutes before filling them with jam, remove the jars from the water and invert them on a clean towel.

6. Place the lids (but not the rings) in a small pan of simmering water until the jars are ready to seal.

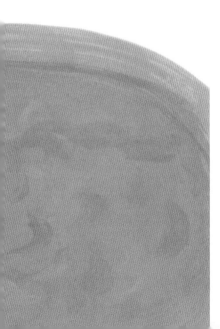

Then make the jam:

· *Bring a large pot of water to a rapid boil. A few at a time, drop the whole plums into the boiling water for about a minute. With a large slotted spoon, remove the plums to a towel to cool.*

· *When cool enough to handle, slip the skins from the plums and discard. Remove the seeds and puree the flesh in a food processor until smooth.*

· *In a heavy 3-quart saucepan, combine 3 cups of the plum pulp and 3 cups of sugar. (If you have less pulp, simply add an equal amount of sugar. If you have more, cook the jam in multiple batches).*

· *Bring to a full boil over high heat, stirring constantly. Boil for 7 or 8 minutes, or until the jam thickly clings to the back of a metal spoon. Remove from the heat and skim the foam off the top.*

· *Pour the jam into the prepared jars, and carefully wipe the rims, sides, and edges with a damp cloth. With tongs, lift the lids from the simmering water, dry them, and place on the clean jar tops. Screw the rings on tightly and set the jars aside to cool. You will hear a popping sound when the lids seal.*

· *Let the jars sit for at least 8 hours, and preferably overnight, to allow them to properly gel. If any jars do not seal, put them in the refrigerator and use that jam first.*

Mom's Pumpkin Cake

*T*he smell and taste of this sweet treat define the holidays for me. Although canned pumpkin can be used, this recipe is an excellent use for the pumpkins that ripen after jack-o'-lantern time.

Makes 2 loaves

3 1/3 cups flour

3 cups sugar

1/2 teaspoon baking powder

2 teaspoons baking soda

1 1/2 teaspoons salt

1 teaspoon ground cinnamon

1/2 teaspoon ground cloves

1 cup chopped walnuts or pecans

1 1/3 cups raisins

2 cups pumpkin puree

2/3 cup softened butter

2 large eggs

2/3 cup water

· *Preheat the oven to 325°.*

· *Into a large mixing bowl, sift the flour, sugar, baking powder, baking soda, salt, cinnamon, and cloves. Add the nuts, raisins, pumpkin, butter, eggs, and water. Using an electric mixer, thoroughly combine the ingredients without over-beating.*

· *Pour into 2 well-greased medium loaf pans and bake for 1 to 1 1/2 hours, or until a toothpick inserted in the center comes out clean. Cool in the pans for 10 minutes, and then remove to a wire rack to cool completely before cutting.*

· *Serve plain or with freshly-whipped cream. Store at room temperature for up to 1 week, or wrap tightly and freeze for up to 6 months.*

Raspberry Chambord Dressing

After experiencing the delicious pleasure of Chambord on vanilla ice cream, I decided to find other ways to use this tasty liqueur. This dressing hits the mark, especially when toasted walnuts top off the salad.

Makes 1 cup

3/4 cup thawed frozen or fresh raspberries

1/3 cup canola or olive oil

1/3 cup white rice vinegar

2 teaspoons sugar

Dash salt

2 Tablespoons Chambord (optional)

› *Puree the raspberries in a food processor. Pour puree into a cheesecloth-lined strainer set over a jar or bowl. Using a rubber spatula, gently press the puree through the strainer to remove the seeds.*

› *Using a whisk, mix in the oil, vinegar, sugar, and salt. Stir in the Chambord.*

› *Chill, and serve over greens or as a sauce for cold meats.*

Rick's Favorite Pepper Relish

*F*ollowing a trip to the pick-your-own vegetable farms in Willcox, Arizona, I had to find creative uses for many boxes of freshly-picked bell peppers. This recipe was a hit, and over time it has evolved into this appetizing version.

Makes about 6 pints

12 to 15 medium green, red, or yellow bell peppers, stems and seeds removed

6 medium white or yellow onions, peeled

1 1/2 cups white sugar

1 cup apple cider vinegar

2 teaspoons kosher or sea salt

› *Coarsely chop the peppers and onions by hand, or by small batches in a food processor. Line a large strainer or colander with cheesecloth and drain the vegetables overnight.*

› *Place the vegetables in a large glass bowl, cover with boiling water, and let them stand for 5 minutes. Drain again, and place the mixture in a 3-quart saucepan, along with the sugar, vinegar, and salt. Over high heat, bring the relish to a boil, reduce the heat and simmer for 20 minutes.*

› *Meanwhile, prepare 6 pint jars according to the instructions on page 88.*

› *Ladle relish into hot, sterilized jars, seal, and store for a month before using. Properly sealed jars keep for up to 1 year in a cool, dark place.*

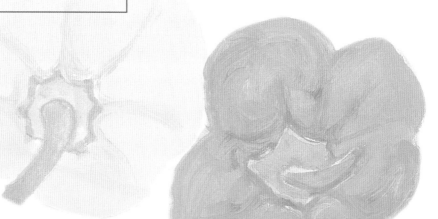

Salsa Fresca

*I*t's not spring and summer in the Southwest without this delicious and foolproof fresh salsa made from tomatoes, onions, peppers, and cilantro.

Makes about 1 quart

1 cup cilantro leaves, washed and removed from stems

3 cups finely-chopped tomatoes (do not use a food processor)

1 large white or yellow onion, chopped finely

5 or 6 small green onions, chopped finely

2 small jalapeño peppers, seeded and minced

Juice of one lime

Salt to taste

· *With a very sharp knife, chop the cilantro leaves quite finely, and then place them in a bowl with the other ingredients. Add the salt a pinch or two at a time, stirring in and tasting after each addition until the flavor is balanced.*

· *Serve this salsa with chips, on eggs, in tacos or burros, or as a spicy addition to a tossed green salad dressed with vinaigrette.*

· *Use within two days for peak flavor. After that time, mix any remaining salsa with steamed brown or white rice, sprinkle with finely grated cheddar cheese, and serve as a side dish.*

Simple Dill Pickles

After eating these pickles at a favorite deli in Palm Springs, I had to recreate the fresh taste at home. Although not exactly the same, this is a tasty rendition.

Makes about 1 quart

1 pound freshly-picked cucumbers

1 Tablespoon pickling salt or table salt

1 large white onion

Fresh dill sprigs or 1 Tablespoon dried dill

2 cups white vinegar

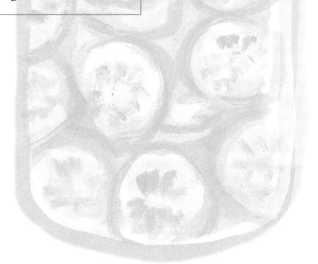

· *Slice the cucumbers as thinly as possible, and layer them with the salt in a strainer. Let sit for about an hour.*

· *Rinse and drain the cucumbers, then place them between layers of clean, lint-free toweling, and press to dry.*

· *Peel and thinly slice the onion, then layer it with the cucumbers and the dill in a nonreactive jar or covered dish. Add the vinegar and refrigerate.*

· *The pickles can be eaten almost immediately, but they will mellow in flavor in about 2 weeks. They keep for several months in the refrigerator.*

Southwestern Gazpacho

*I*f you like salsa, you'll love this spicy twist on an old favorite.

Serves 6

6 to 8 ripe tomatoes

1 large green or yellow bell pepper, cored, seeded, and chopped

1 small hot pepper, such as Anaheim, jalapeño, or serrano, seeded and minced

3 green or bunching onions, including greens, chopped

1 large cucumber, peeled, seeded, and diced

1 clove fresh garlic, minced

1/2 cup finely chopped basil leaves

1/2 cup finely chopped cilantro leaves

1/2 cup extra virgin olive oil

Juice of 2 limes (lemon may be substituted)

3 cups chilled chicken or vegetable stock

Salt to taste

Sour cream

Croutons

› *Bring a 2-quart saucepan full of water to a boil, and carefully add the tomatoes 1 at a time for about 30 seconds each. Remove them with a large slotted spoon and place them on a towel.*

› *When they are cool enough to handle, remove the cores, and slip the skin off each tomato. Cut them into quarters, remove the seeds with your thumbs, and chop the remaining flesh.*

› *Place the tomatoes, chopped bell peppers, minced hot pepper, chopped onions, diced cucumber, and minced garlic in a large bowl and gently mix together. Stir in the chopped basil and cilantro leaves, along with the olive oil, juice, and stock.*

› *Refrigerate for at least 2 hours, and then add the salt a pinch at a time, tasting after each addition.*

› *To serve, ladle the soup into chilled bowls. Top with a dollop of sour cream and a few croutons.*

Recommended Seed Companies

Burpee

300 Park Avenue
Warminster PA 18991-0008
Phone: (800) 888-1447
Web Page: http://www.burpee.com

Cook's Garden

P.O. Box 535
Londonderry VT 05148
Phone: (800) 457-9703
Web Page: http://www.cooksgarden.com

High Country Gardens

2902 Rufina Street
Santa Fe NM 85707-2929
Phone: (800) 925-9387
Web Page: http://www.highcountrygardens.com

Kitchen Garden Seeds

23 Tulip Drive
Bantam CT 06750-6086
Phone: (860) 567-6086
Web Page: http://www.kitchengardenseeds.com

Native Seeds/SEARCH

526 N. Fourth Avenue
Tucson AZ 85705
Phone: (520) 622-5561
Web Page: http://www.nativeseeds.org

Plants of the Southwest

3095 Agua Fria
Santa Fe NM 87507
Phone: (800) 788-7333
Web Page: http://www.plantsofthesouthwest.com

Roswell Seed Company

P.O. Box 725
Roswell NM 88202-0725
Phone: (505) 622-7701

Seeds of Change

P.O. Box 15700
Santa Fe NM 87506
(888) 762-7333
Web Page: http://www.seedsofchange.com

Shepherd's Garden Seeds

30 Irene Street
Torrington CT 06790-6658
Phone: (800) 503-9624
Web Page: http://www.shepherdseeds.com

Index